is familiar with us and knows just who we are." It appears at its most repellent in the cuteness and vulgarity of much advertising copy, but has also infected some recent fiction. "Stuffiness," as Mr. Gibson labels the impersonal rhetoric of officialese and the jargon of specialists, is the self-protective response of a writer who withdraws from uncertainty into an "omniscient and polysyllabic detachment."

All three styles are defined by listing specific preferences in vocabulary, grammar, and syntax. Of particular interest are the appendices, which succeed admirably in explaining precisely how impressions of personality derived from style may be accounted for in concrete rhetorical terms. In analyzing the choices writers make, and their results, Mr. Gibson has used the tools of scientific linguistics and added to them by bringing to bear on modern prose his own lively and perceptive mind.

WALKER GIBSON, Professor of English at New York University, is the author of *Seeing and Writing* and *The Limits of Language*, as well as many articles on the subject of composition. His poetry has appeared in the *New Yorker, Harper's,* and the *Nation,* and in two collections, *The Reckless Spenders* and *Come as You Are*. His analysis of contemporary styles was stimulated by his experiences as a writer and a teacher of creative writing.

TOUGH, SWEET AND STUFFY

WALKER GIBSON

Tough, *Sweet* & Stuffy

AN ESSAY ON MODERN AMERICAN PROSE STYLES

INDIANA UNIVERSITY PRESS

BLOOMINGTON & LONDON

TO NANCY

Let the truth be said outright: there are no synonyms, and the same statement can never be repeated in a changed form of words.

—Walter Raleigh, *Style* (1897)

CONTENTS

vii

PREFACE

As Rhetoric is intended to be judged . . . it must necessarily be our object not only to render speech demonstrative and credible, but also to produce a particular
impression in our judges. For . . . it is a highly important
element of proof that the speaker should enjoy the credit
of a certain character and should be disposed by his
audience to stand in a certain relation to themselves,
and further that the audience in their turn should, if
possible, have a particular disposition to the speaker.
—Aristotle's *Rhetoric* (Welldon translation)

This is not a guidebook for improving one's style of
writing, though it does offer in its final chapter some
Practical Advice. Nor is it a history or survey of prose
styles, useful though these might be. It is an essay—an
attempt—to describe three extreme but familiar styles in
modern American prose. I call these three styles Tough
Talk, Sweet Talk, and Stuffy Talk.

What I mean by Tough Talk is most easily discovered
in works of fiction where a narrator-hero identifies himself as a hard man who has been around. By Sweet Talk I
refer primarily to the blandishments of advertising. And
Stuffy Talk, of course, suggests the hollow tones of officialese. But as my Style Sampler in the appendix demon-

strates, the three styles are by no means confined to these genres of writing. And obviously, not all modern novels are Tough, not all ads are Sweet, not all official prose is Stuffy. Traces of the three styles appear, I shall argue, in the language of everything we write, where they stand for decisions we have made about how to place ourselves before a reader.

When a writer selects a style, however unconsciously, and so presents himself to a reader, he chooses certain words and not others, and he prefers certain organizations of words to other possible organizations. I take it that every choice he makes is significant in dramatizing a personality or voice, with a particular center of concern and a particular relation to the person he is addressing. Such self-dramatizations in language are what I mean by style. The Tough Talker, in these terms, is a man dramatized as centrally concerned with himself—his style is *I*-talk. The Sweet Talker goes out of his way to be nice to us—his is style is *you*-talk. The Stuffy Talker expresses no concern either for himself or his reader—his style is *it*-talk. These are three extreme possibilities: the way we write at any given moment can be seen as an adjustment or compromise among these three styles of identifying ourselves and defining our relation with others.

The quotation from the Greek sage at the head of this preface is not intended solely to lend weight to a sometimes airy argument—though that is certainly part of its purpose. It is also a reminder that there is nothing new in the obligation "to produce a particular impression of ourselves and a particular disposition in our judges." My omissions in the passage may obscure the fact that Aristotle was really talking about political oratory and courtroom pleading. But the need to produce a particular impression of ourselves, "to enjoy the credit of a certain character," affects every moment of social behavior. Rhetoric, says Aristotle, is intended to be judged. The purpose of this essay is to begin asking how, in our time, character is created by rhetoric.

Any answer to such a question requires the most concrete possible examination of words and their arrangements in sentences and paragraphs. Yet the reader who is up on such things will note that I carry on the discussion here with only passing reliance on the "new grammars"—structural, transformational, or whatever. Partly I have my own ignorance to blame; partly too the restriction is deliberate. Many of the distinctions I am seeking can be defined in the familiar terms we all learned in school, and if you can remember what a subordinate clause is, you have most of the expertise this book demands. The reader I have most in mind, then, is not "up on such things" at all—he is an interested layman concerned about modern uses of prose. Or he is a teacher or student for whom these pages may offer "further reading" in his courses in composition or literary criticism. Above all, he is a part-time reader and writer who would like to think further about his own life with language.

But my reliance (with exceptions) on the familiar vocabulary of traditional grammar must not be misleading. The fact is that a great deal is going on right now in the study of language, and some of it is certain to contribute to the study of style. Already there are figures on the frontier—I think particularly of Francis Christensen and Richard Ohmann—whose efforts to relate style to the fresh approaches of transformational grammar look exceedingly hopeful. Meanwhile it is possible that this essay may support their exertions, while introducing my general reader to some of his powers and responsibilities as a user of words.

Most of this study was completed during a year in which I enjoyed sabbatical leave from New York University and a Fellowship from the John Simon Guggenheim Foundation. I am grateful for the generosity of both these amiable institutions. The suggestions of Professor Sheridan Baker of the University of Michigan on an early manuscript were most helpful.

W. G.

TOUGH, SWEET AND STUFFY

1

INTRODUCTIONS
Meeting People in Daily Life
and in Prose

To prepare a face to meet the faces that you meet.

It may be helpful to begin a study of verbal style by reminding ourselves how much we experience, and how much we communicate with one another, in ways that are not verbal at all. Consider for example the familiar moment, in the ordinary course of social or business life, when we are introduced to a new acquaintance. Like most of human experience, it is a moment susceptible to a more complex description than we usually grant it. Facing a new face, we make a series of judgments based on a large range of half-conscious, and nonverbal, sense impressions. The words uttered by our new acquaintance —how do you do?—may be banal enough, but the physical voice that utters them is rich in meaning, just as the physical appearance of the person we are confronting is open to immediate, and of course potentially faulty, interpretation. Is he friend or foe? One to be encouraged as an attractive addition to life, or a threat to our own dearly-beloved ego? Can I handle him or will he handle me? We begin answering such questions immediately at the point of confrontation, and even though we know the tentative quality of our answers, having learned our lesson about snap judgments, we make them anyway. For we are bombarded with impressions of such power and meaning that to ignore them we would have to be a clod, or an extremely well-disciplined and reserved sensibility.

Suppose we consider some of these impressions.

First there are matters of sheer physique. Is our new acquaintance taller than we are? Shorter? The same? What does this imply about our *standing* vis-à-vis one another? (Can anyone claim to be quite oblivious to this distinction, for all its savagery? When we *look up to* or *down on* someone else, we may do so metaphorically or we may do so literally, but often we do both.) Do we associate this person's bigness, furthermore, with the character of the bully, or with that easygoing good nature of the large mind in a large body? Or neither? If he is small, do we associate his smallness with some sort of anxious inferiority, or rather an attractive delicacy or refinement? Or something else? Our fleeting judgments here, and our consequent adjustments of our own behavior, are based in part, no doubt, on some dim past experience of tallness and smallness, but, more to the point, on a large number of other physical impressions that we quickly gather in at the moment. The manner of dress, the cut of the hair, the depth of the eyes, the grasp of the hand, the significant contortions of the mouth as it politely smiles (or as it doesn't) — all these and a dozen other physical impressions, with their inevitable associations, color our split-second response, to be filed away for corroboration or correction in the light of further evidence.

There follows an auditory impression—the four words (for

instance), How do you do. There are ways of saying those four words, reinforced by appropriate facial expression and perhaps gesture, that express hostility, or boredom, or irrepressible self-satisfaction; just as there are other ways that express eagerness to be of service, gay amiability, or a readiness for a grand passion.[1] The way a person says "How do you do," and the way he looks and behaves as he does so, are combined and interfused in practice, so that we hear a voice and feel a grip and see a facial expression all in one muddle of sensation. Sometimes we even smell things. And it is next to impossible to feel neutral about these matters, though we may try to *think* neutral. The most we can do is reserve our impressions with as much readiness for correction as possible. I dislike this fellow, but then some of my best friends have had these shaggy eyebrows and this unctuous manner. Or: I do find this person attractive, but then I remember all the smiles like this one that have turned out to be empty after all.

The familiar social moment I have been discussing can be looked at as well from our own point of view, as an *actor* in the situation. We too are eager to "make an impression," consciously or not. During that first moment of meeting a new individual, we adopt a posture more or less deliberately calculated to express a *self* with a relation (friendliness, reserve, hostility, boredom) toward the other person. The motives and impulses that prompt us to adopt this or that role and relation are mysterious in the extreme; they must lie somewhere in the very depths of personality. In any event they certainly lie beyond the bounds of this study. What is obvious enough, though, in our practice of taking a role in a social situation, is the great variety of resources that we have at our disposal, to make our posture work. Even our preparations were elaborate, and significant. We dressed that

morning in a certain way, presumably from personal choice
to some extent, and our "choice" was a choice of an exterior
face to confront the world with, a role to play. We parted our
hair and tied a necktie—or we didn't. We have grown a beard,
or a mustache, or we have not. For a woman, the term *make-
up* well describes one part of her self-expression. We are all
makers-up, with or without cosmetics. Once on the scene,
the situation of how-do-you-do, we may use a wide variety
of techniques for further dramatizing the self. The shrug of
a shoulder, the lift of an eyebrow, the tilt of the head—all
these are familiar, perhaps automatic, expressions of personality. Then there are people who stolidly refrain from such
activity—they just stand there—and this too is literally *self*-
explanatory. Our way of managing our voice is of course
enormously important, quite aside from any verbal message
and quite aside from the inherent virtues of our voice-box
itself. We may be naturally endowed with a voice of richness
and beauty, or with a quavering falsetto, but these gifts are
less important than our immediate meaningful control of
voice on the scene of action. Visual maneuvering of our lips
can also impress, and between the sneer of disdain and the
smile of invitation there are a hundred subtle elaborations.
What we do with our eyes, beyond simply meeting another's
eyes, says much. It is, in sum, a considerable battery of
weapons we have at our command, and beside it the actual
words we may stammer forth look pale indeed. How do you
do? Yes, isn't it a pleasant day.[2]

Life is not always lived, fortunately, at this rather brutally
physical level. Eventually, often, people do say things to one
another, and the things they say matter. Words do count.
Yet even in our most successful and reasonable conversations,
our words are footnoted, supported, even contradicted by our

bodies and our dumb feelings, by a whole complex of details in the situation. No doubt these distractions (if that is what they are) diminish with longer acquaintance. Still, when someone tells us something, no matter how well we may know him, how adjusted to his appearance we may be, our understanding of his meaning is almost certainly more than verbal, involving a sense of the *him* that is talking, at the moment, in the flesh, before us.

A simple experiment has been tried with a tape recorder, to suggest some of these influences in communication. A recording is made of an ordinary social conversation among several friends. Then a written version is transcribed from the recording, and distributed to people not present at the occasion. To them the typescript is likely to seem not only dull and lifeless, but in places actually mysterious, incomprehensible. The tape recording is then played, and the conversation begins to take on color and interest, while ambiguities are often cleared up by inflection and tone of voice. Personalities emerge, conflicts become apparent that a reading of the words on paper could not identify. But of course it is still a very pale expression of the experience. What would be needed to render the conversation with some verisimilitude would be several television cameras in color, a highly skilled director, and a video tape reproducing gesture, facial expression, clothing, and physique. But even then . . .

Communication, whatever it is, is more than a matter of words, and in some familiar situations it is a great deal more than words. When in ordinary social and business life we identify ourselves before others (or indeed before ourselves), when we convey attitudes and information, when we take in the intentions of our fellow creatures, we use several of our senses at once, and we use them in complicated ways. We are *present*, clothed and combed, three-dimensional, taking up space and filling the air with our peculiar personal accents. We present ourselves by being present. The fact that we do this, as often as not, with nonchalant ease should not obscure the variety and richness of our communicating.[3]

The distinction I am working toward should be obvious enough. *The writer is not physically present to his reader*. He is all words. The writer has no resources at all for dramatizing himself and his message to his reader except those scratches on paper—he has no bulk, no audible voice on the airwaves, no way of introducing himself beyond what he can make his reader "see" by means of abstract written words in various arrangements. To these words the reader responds much as he responds in a social situation—that is, he infers a personality—but he has only words to go on. Therefore the writer's particular choices of words as he makes his introduction in prose have an absolute kind of importance and finality. His reader is by no means so ready to reserve judgment, to wait and see, as a new social acquaintance. A reader can shut the book at any moment, at the slightest displeasure. Measured against the ordinary social life of meeting and speaking, the writer's handicaps seem enormous. Measured against almost any other medium of communication we can think of, the written language suffers by comparison, in respect to flexibility and directness and power of expression. Compared with an obviously limited device like the telephone, for instance, the written document has several advantages—such as portability, easy duplication, a wider vocabulary, and the possibility of careful preparation—but the dramatizing of a self may be easier on the phone, for all one's physical removal from the listener. The exact degree of reluctance that any native speaker of English can put into his enunciation of the syllable "we-e-ell" over a telephone wire is exceedingly difficult for the writer to duplicate without a great many words and a great deal of skill. A businessman deciding whether to pursue a particular operation by phone or by letter may choose the letter as more suited to his immediate situation. It can be revised before mailing, and filed after. But if it is direct personal force that he wants to employ, the power of a dramatized personality with the ability to adjust immediately to the other's response, then he will certainly choose the phone. Or better still, he will ask his man to lunch.

Yet surely I am not defending the telephone or the lunch table over the written word. Surely there is something wrong-headed in what I have been saying. It may be, as many modern linguists have been saying, and to much good effect, that the written language is merely a "dialect" of the spoken language, and an overrated one at that.[4] But if those black marks on paper suffer great handicaps—as they do—without lips or eyes or voiceboxes, without gesture or the presence of a physical speaker, how is it that some of the finest characters we know come from books? And by "characters" here I do not mean people like Hamlet or Mr. Micawber, admirable though these are, but the *voices* that address us in written prose. Somehow or other, the writer is able to compensate for his handicaps, exploit his advantages, and *introduce* himself to us in a special role. That is part of his skill, part of his art. My effort in this study is to translate that phrase "somehow or other" into terms a little less desperately vague, by asking how, especially in brief opening passages, words have been chosen and arranged to introduce a character talking to us.

But before going further, we ought to ask, Who is being introduced in a piece of prose, and to whom? These are sticky critical problems of long standing. Is the writer himself saying how do you do? There is a sense in which he certainly is, but most statements about an author's self-revelation in his works (especially works of fiction) are naive. It is one of his selves at best, one of his possible voices, one of his roles, that he is introducing us to. The problem is posed most clearly when, in fiction, we are presented to a narrator who is "worlds apart" from his creator and from us. The speaker we are introduced to in *Huckleberry Finn* is obviously not Mark Twain, whoever he was, or Samuel L. Clemens, whoever *he* was. Nor is it Huck himself, exactly, for though we hear the voice of Huck talking to us, we are well aware that there is somebody else very much in the wings, somebody superior to Huck intellectually while sympathetic with him morally. It is as if we were exchanging glances over Huck's head with this somebody, who is "more like us," while Huck babbles on. This other person can be called "Mark Twain" in a loose sort of way, but as scholarship has shown, *and would show about anybody,* Mr. Clemens the Real Man had a bewildering number of voices, moods, grievances, problems, selves. It would be better to use a term like "the implied author" or "the author's second self" to suggest the restricted, artificial role that the real-life writer creates to stand behind his also-created first-person-narrator.[5] In *Huck* this "second self" is a very genial fellow indeed, who can even refer comfortably to his "own" name, or can make his narrator do so:

You don't know about me without you have read a book by the name of *The Adventures of Tom Sawyer,* but that ain't no matter. That book was made by Mr. Mark Twain and he told the truth mainly. There was things he stretched, but mainly he told the truth.

There is a story by Ring Lardner called "Haircut" which has won more notoriety for its radical narrative technique than for its worth as a story. Here the "other self" behind the narrator is superior both intellectually *and* morally to the barber who tells the story, and who condemns himself in our eyes by the things he says and the way he says them. But is this "other self" Lardner, this wiser intelligence who, with us, sees through the barber's crudities and cruelties? Possibly, in a way. Possibly, while he was writing the story. But anyone acquainted with authors knows that they are just as mysterious and changeable as the rest of us. When, for instance, a writer repudiates one of his early works, it is probable, not that he has lost sympathy with his narrator, but that he has lost sympathy with the "second self" controlling the narrator. Lardner might well have come to feel, in the case of his oft-cited story, that the second self in "Haircut" is a rather oversimple fellow. And he is. Narrators, after all, are relatively fixed; they end when the story ends; authors can change their minds and grow up.

In any case it seems useful to recognize that in most first-person-singular accounts of events we are really dealing with two voices, one that of the narrator, the other that of the second self, the Assumed Author, the Creator-Identity, or what you will. Nor is this doubleness confined to fiction. A man writing an autobiography, or even a letter, has the same problem. He poses an "I" doing the talking, and implies another "I" wryly or comfortably or even tragically standing back of the narrator. Behind both of these, of course, stands the true-to-life Real-Life-Writer, who is a mass of chemistry, nerve-endings, and irrelevance. *His* intentions are mixed and mysterious—to make money, finish his difficult paragraph, have dinner, who knows?

In practice, as I hope we shall see below, we can make critical progress by confining ourselves largely to the narrator alone, the person doing the talking. In most prose it is this voice that we take to be that of the assumed author, the writer's second self. (Besides, there is good reason not to overcomplicate the experience of reading by trying to talk about too many people trying to talk at once!) Still, there often remains the question of how "seriously" we are to take a given narrator, how thoroughly we are expected (and by whom?) to endorse and approve of his statements. Difficulties of this sort have been increasing in twentieth-century fiction, where the relation between narrator (especially a first-person narrator) and second self is left deliberately obscure. In *Huck*, we have no doubt that we are to sympathize morally with Huck's attitudes and to laugh tolerantly at his language. But *The Adventures of Augie March*, among many others, poses a more complex situation for the reader, who is really unsure how far he is expected to press his sympathy for Augie, that exuberant grab-bag mixture of virtues and weaknesses, of learned and lowbrow languages. We shall face this problem more directly when, in Chapter 5, we are introduced to Augie in person.

The experience of reading, then, is a confrontation with a voice, or personality, clear or confused—a personality who by means of words on paper gets himself *introduced* to us. But what about *us*, the reader? It is not generally understood that the reader too, like the author, undergoes a transformation, that he too becomes a kind of ideal or second self as he exposes himself to the expectations of the language. Early in his career Henry James argued that an author has to "make his reader very much as he makes his characters," and this is quite literally true. As readers, we are made over every time we take up a piece of writing: we recognize that there are assumptions and expectations implied there and that as sympathetic listeners to the voice speaking to us, we must share these assumptions. Sophisticated readers are able to move in this manner in several directions, and to keep separate their true-life personalities from the roles that the language is temporarily asking them to play. Thus, to mention obvious examples, it is possible for nonbelievers to be successful readers of *Paradise Lost* or the poems of Hopkins; it is possible, with one of one's selves, to suffer the appropriate moral agonies posed by a Victorian novel, while at the same time recognizing that in one's true-life self, facing a similar situation in a true-life world, one would adopt another point of view. Much of the force of modern advertising comes from the writer's skill in defining a particular set of ideal characteristics with which the confused real reader may be expected to desire identification. Some of the rhetoric involved in "getting sold" will concern us in Chapter 6.

In all our reading, however, it is vital for us to maintain clearly a distinction between ourselves as real people acting in a real world, on the one hand, and ourselves as that particular bundle of assumed values that any piece of language implies. This, in the case of advertising, is the way we keep our money in our pockets. In the case of polemical writing, it is the way we keep from changing our party with every word we read. In the case of fiction, it is the way we keep from imposing the values of art too crudely on the problems of life.[6]

In what follows, I shall be asking how writers introduce themselves in those crucial opening paragraphs of prose works. How, that is to say, they present to us a *self*, the assumed author, not to be confused with that complex mass of chaotic experience making up the writer as human being. The procedure can be simple enough. Of the beginnings of assorted prose works, let us ask: (1) Who's talking? Who is being introduced? (2) To whom is he being introduced? Who are *we* expected to be as we read this prose sympathetically? (3) By what magic was all this done? How were words chosen and arranged in order to make these effects possible, without physical voice, or gesture, or facial expression?

By such a process, I hope to define three kinds of personality that seem to me recognizable in modern American prose. These personalities I call the Tough Talker, the Sweet Talker, and the Stuffy Talker. I will be examining some extreme forms of their three styles of talk, to make identification and definition possible. But my proposal is that all prose (including this sentence) can be looked at as an adjustment or compromise of some sort among these three possible ways of addressing the reader.

2

HEARING VOICES
Tough Talk, Sweet Talk, Stuffy Talk

It ain't what ya do,
Hit's the way that ya do it,
That's what gets results.

Suppose we begin to read—to expose ourselves to an introduction.

Suppose we pick up, for instance, a magazine, the *Saturday Review*. We riffle its pages. Already we are taking on some attributes of an assumed reader: we have some experience of this magazine and its general personality, and we know vaguely the sort of person we are expected to be as we read it. We are not, at any rate, at this moment, the assumed reader of *The Hudson Review*, or *The New Yorker*, or *House Beautiful*, or *Frisky Stories*. The eye lights on a title. Just our subject. Who's speaking here?

THE PRIVATE WORLD OF A MAN WITH A BOOK

The temptation of the educator is to explain and describe, to organize a body of knowledge for the student, leaving the student with nothing to do. I have never been able to understand why educators do this so often, especially where books are concerned.

Much of this time they force their students to read the wrong books at the wrong time, and insist that they read them in the wrong way. That is, they lecture to the students about what is in the books, reduce the content to a series of points that can be remembered, and, if there are discussions, arrange them to deal with the points.

Schools and colleges thus empty books of their true meaning, and addict their students to habits of thought that often last for the rest of their lives. Everything must be reduced to a summary, ideas are topic sentences, to read is to prepare for a distant test. This is why so many people do not know how to read. They have been taught to turn books into abstractions.[1]

Everything depends on the *personality* to whom we have just been introduced. His message can never be divorced from that personality, that speaking voice—or at least not without becoming essentially another message. The question I am asking is not "What is he saying?" but "Who is he? What sort of person am I being asked to *be*, as I experience these words?" A difficulty immediately arises. We can hardly describe with justice the fellow talking except by quoting his own words. He is what he says, precisely. The minute we lift an assumed "I" out of the text and start to describe or reproduce his personality in *our* language, or in language that we infer might be his, we are admittedly altering him, mangling him, killing him perhaps. But it is the only way. The biologist studing cellular structure has to dye his specimen under the microscope so he can see its parts, but the dye kills the living tissue, and what he sees is dead and gone. It is a familiar intellectual dilemma, and there is nothing to do but be cheerful about it, applying one's dye as liberally as necessary while recognizing its poisonous possibilities.

With that proviso, then, who's talking, in the first two paragraphs of "The Private World of a Man with a Book"?

What assumptions is he sharing with his ideal reader? What follows is, as I hear it, a between-the-lines communication between the assumed author and the assumed reader:

You and I know all about the shoddy academic situation, where lazy and wrongheaded teachers do so much harm to the true meaning of books. You and I share a true knowledge of true meanings, and can recognize instantly when wrong books are taught at the wrong time in the wrong way. I am a rugged no-nonsense character, for all my academic connections, and you, thrusting out your jaw, couldn't agree more.

Now it is clear from this effort that I (the assumed author of this essay) do not very successfully engage myself as the ideal assumed reader of these two paragraphs. It is clear that when I have the speaker saying "You and I share a true knowledge of true meanings" I am not writing a paraphrase at all, but a parody. I am exaggerating what I take to be a sort of arrogance in the speaker, with a view to ridicule. How did I reach this curious position?

I reached it because, as I read the two paragraphs, I suffered a conflict. I was aware, on the one hand, of the person I was supposed to be (one who knows what "true meanings" are, for instance). But I was also aware, much too aware, that I was *not* that person, and, more important, didn't want to pretend to be. This is not a question of changing one's beliefs for the sake of a literary experience—that is easy enough. One can "become" a Hindu or a Hottentot if the speaker is sufficiently persuasive and attractive. But that's the rub: the speaker must be attractive to us. And in this case, because of qualities I have called "arrogance" and "rugged no-nonsense," I have become not the assumed reader at all, but a hostile reader.[2] Consider one moment where hostility, at least in this reader, was aroused. It is the second sentence—"I have

never been able to understand why educators do this. . . ."
The difficulty here is that we sense hypocrisy in that remark.
Just how is the assumed reader being addressed? Is it this?

I've tried and tried to understand why teachers go at books this
way, but I just can't get it.

Or is it this?

The trouble with teachers is that they're either too dim-witted or
too lazy to teach books the right way. Oh I understand it all right!

Now which is it? Let's admit it could be either (a fault in itself?), but insofar as we may strongly suspect it's the second,
then the actual phrasing ("I have never been able to understand") seems falsely prevaricating in its covert antagonism.

I have used such expressions as "rugged no-nonsense," "covert antagonism," and "thrusting out your jaw." In the next-
to-last sentence of our passage we can illustrate one rhetorical
technique by which impressions like these are conveyed. "This
is why so many people do not know how to read." We have
here, to anticipate, some rhetoric of Tough Talk. The phrasing does not allow the possibility that not so many people are
so benighted after all. No doubts are permitted. By placing
its "many people do not know how to read" in a subordinate
clause, the voice assumes a *fact* from what is at best an extreme
statement of an arguable position. The independent clause
("This is why") merely speculates on the cause of the "fact."
The reader is pushed around by a tough-talking voice.

But insofar as we can divorce the utterance here from the
utterer—and I have said that this is strictly impossible—then
what is being said in this paragraph seems to me both true and
important. Indeed, I would personally agree, books *are* too

often taught as abstractions, and in any vote in any faculty meeting, the assumed author and this reader would vote together on this issue. But we do not take pleasure in reading for such reasons as that. In fact it may have been this very agreement, this sense that I personally did not need persuading, that led me to read no further in the article than the two paragraphs I have quoted. But surely it was not only that. I read no more because I felt that the assumed author was browbeating me, and changing me over in ways I did not like. I don't care how "right" he is: he's got to be *nice* to me!

But unfortunately, it is not enough to be nice. Life is very hard. Let us consider now another assumed author—same magazine, a few years earlier, same general subject—and listen to a voice that goes out of its way to be nice.

UNREQUIRED READING

The title of this essay may strike you as a typographical error. You may be saying to yourself that the writer really means required reading, and the phrase conjures up for you, I suspect, lists distributed on the first days of college courses: Volume One of this distinguished scholar's work on the Byzantine empire in the fourth century, that brochure on the economic interpretation of the Constitution, this pundit's principles of economics, that pedant's source book.

Or, perhaps, still under the apprehension that I mean required reading, you are reminded of what by now is one of the more maddening insolences of criticism, or at any rate of book reviewing. "'This,' says Mr. Notability, "is a *must* book." This in the atomic age is compulsory reading. In a world of anxiety this uneasy novel is not to be passed by.

I beg of you to forget such obligations and responsibilities. To this day you have to forget that you *had* to read "Macbeth" in order to begin to remember how perturbingly moving a play it is. Hardly anyone would reread Burke's "Speech on Conciliation" if he recalled how he had to make an abstract of it in high school.[3]

Once again let us try to assess the sort of person addressing us here, remembering that this person bears no necessary connection with its author. In listening to this voice, we become aware as always of an ideal listener, a "you," whose characteristics we are expected to adopt as we read.

I am a sweet professorish sort of fellow, full of big words but simple at heart—you are younger than I, and though you have of course been through college, you are by no means an academic professional like me. My charm is based on an old-fashioned sort of formality ("I beg of you") combined with a direct conversational approach that I trust you find attractive. I wear my learning lightly, occasionally even offering you a tricky phrasing *(pundit's principles, pedant's source book)* or a modern cliché *(world of anxiety)* to show you I'm human. But we share, you and I, a knowledgeable experience of literature; we both recognize for example how "perturbingly moving" *Macbeth* really is.

It is easy to identify at least one rhetorical device by which the professorial voice is often dramatized. It is the device of parallel structure. A pattern of balanced phrasings suggests a world similarly balanced, well ordered, academic. The first paragraph's list is an example: *this distinguished scholar, that brochure, this pundit, that pedant.* A somewhat similar effect occurs later: *this is a must book, this is compulsory reading, this is not to be passed by.* Triplets like that are characteristic of the fancier tones. In the last two sentences we have the balanced device of chiasmus, a criss-cross relation of parallel ideas. The clauses there are arranged in an order of time past, time present, time present, time past.

You have to forget that you *had* to read to remember how perturbingly moving it *is*.

Hardly anyone *would reread* Burke (now) if he recalled how he *had* to make an abstract.

Very neat, literary, elegant. Parallel structure alone, of course, could not produce a sweet-professorish voice. But it can support the meanings of the words, as it does here.

The assumed reader, here as always, is a sympathetic yes man, responding uncritically (yet of course intelligently) to the speaker's invitations. When a reader responds critically, in the negative sense, and begins to disagree, he forsakes his role as assumed reader and lets his Real-Life Self take over. If this goes on very long, he will simply stop reading, unless he has some strong motive for swallowing his irritation and continuing.

We can imagine a sympathetic conversation going on between speaker and assumed reader in our passage, something like this:

The title of this essay may strike you as a typographical error. [Why, yes, as a matter of fact it did.] You may be saying to yourself that the writer really means required reading [I did rather think that, yes], and the phrase conjures up for you, I suspect, lists distributed on the first days of college courses [Oh yes, those dreadful things]: Volume one of this etc. [You certainly have it down pat! And I do appreciate your gentle scorn of pundits and pedants.]

But suppose, once again, that one does not enjoy playing the part of this particular assumed reader. Suppose one is uncomfortably aware of an insupportable gap between one's Own True Self and the role one is here being asked to adopt. Again it is probably obvious that I (still the assumed author of this essay) suffer from just such an uncomfortable awareness. The mechanical and prissy straight man that I have constructed out of the assumed reader reveals my own antagonism, both to him and to the sweet talk of the speaker. Suppose we were to play it my way, and invent a conversation be-

tween the speaking voice and a hostile reader who refused to
take on the required qualities:

> The title of this essay may strike you as a typographical error.
> [Why, no, as a matter fact that never occurred to me.] You may
> be saying to yourself that the writer really means required reading
> [Don't be silly. I would be more surprised to see a title so trite. In
> fact your title embodies just the sort of cute phrase I have learned
> to expect from this middlebrow magazine.] and the phrase con-
> jures up for you, I suspect, lists distributed on the first days of
> college courses [That's a dim memory at best. How old do you
> think I am?]: Volume one of this distinguished etc. etc. [You
> bore me with this lengthy list and your affected effects of sound-
> play.]
>   Or, perhaps, still under the apprehension that I mean required
> reading ["Perhaps" is good. How *could* I be "still" under such an
> apprehension?], you are reminded of what by now is one of the
> more maddening insolences of criticism [You're maddened, not
> I. Calm down.], or at any rate of book reviewing. "This," says Mr.
> Notability, "is a *must* book." [Do even book reviewers use such
> language?] This in the atomic age is compulsory reading. In a
> world of anxiety this uneasy novel is not to be passed by. [I appre-
> ciate you are ironically repeating these tired phrases, but they're
> still tired.]

Now of course this mean trick can be worked by anybody
against almost anything. The assumed reader of this essay,
for example, may so far forget himself as to try it on *me*,
though I deeply hope he doesn't. Again it is important to
emphasize that the argument here is not between two
people disagreeing about an issue. I agree with the educational stand taken here about reading, just as I did with the
similar stand taken in our first passage. *The argument is between two people disagreeing about one another.* And this
time it is not a case of the Tough Talker pushing the reader
around, but a case of the Sweet Talker who condescends and
irritates in a totally different way.

The general subject our two writers have been discussing comes down to something we could call The Teaching of Reading. It is a subject that can easily be confronted in some other voice, of course; in fact it seems to me doubtful that there can be *any* subject which by definition *requires* any particular voice. To illustrate the third of my triumvirate of styles, and to exhibit The Teaching of Reading as attacked with a very different voice, I offer the passage that follows. Again it presents a thesis with which I am quite in agreement—as who is not?

TEACHING LITERATURE

Rapid and coherent development of programs in modern literature has led to the production of excellent materials for study from the earliest years of secondary education through the last of undergraduate study. The sole danger—if it be one, in the opinion of others—lies in easy acceptance of what is well done. The mechanics of mass production can overpower and drive out native creativeness in reflecting on literature and so stop individual interpretation in teaching. We hear a good deal of the dangers to imaginative experience in youth from excesses of visual exposure, and we know that they therefore read much less, in quantity, from longer works of prose and poetry. It may prove to be true, therefore, that in the study of literature the critical authority of the printed page will seem an easy substitute for individual analysis of original texts, first for the teacher and next inevitably for students who have never learned to read, with conscious effort in thinking, through verbal symbols.[4]

After making necessary allowances for a passage ripped from context (for I have had to choose this time a paragraph from inside a work rather than an introduction), the fact remains that this is a Stuffy voice. It is by no means an extreme example of Stuffy Talk, but it is Stuffy enough to be marked off as distinct from the Toughness of "Private World" and the Sweetness of "Unrequired Reading." We become, as we read,

solemn; the brow furrows; perhaps we are a little Stuffy ourselves. This transformation is the direct result of certain
habits of vocabulary and sentence structure by which the
Stuffiness is conveyed. I put off identification of these habits
until we have examined the Tough Talker and Sweet Talker
more thoroughly. Meanwhile, my point is that a *style* is not
simply a response to a particular kind of subject-matter, nor is
it entirely a matter of the writer's situation and his presumed
audience. It is partly a matter of sheer individual will, a desire for a particular kind of self-definition no matter what the
circumstances.

The point can be further illuminated by trying just one
more introduction, asking ourselves what sort of voice this is:

ON TEACHING THE APPRECIATION OF POETRY

I hold no diploma, certificate, or other academic document to
show that I am qualified to discuss this subject. I have never
taught anybody of any age how to enjoy, understand, appreciate
poetry, or how to speak it. I have known a great many poets, and
innumerable people who wanted to be told that they were poets. I
have done some teaching, but I have never "taught poetry." My
excuse for taking up this subject is of a wholly different origin. I
know that not only young people in colleges and universities, but
secondary school children also, have to study, or at least acquaint
themselves with, poems by living poets; and I know that my poems
are among those studied, by two kinds of evidence. My play *Murder in the Cathedral* is a set book in some schools: there is an edition of the English text published in Germany with notes in Ger-
man, and an edition published in Canada with notes in English.
The fact that this play, and some of my other poems, are used in
schools brings some welcome supplement to my income; and it also
brings an increase in my correspondence, which is more or less welcome, though not all letters get answered. These are letters from
the children themselves or more precisely, the teenagers. They live
mostly in Britain, the United States, and Germany, with a sprin-

kling from the nations of Asia. It is in a spirit of curiosity, therefore, that I approach the subject of the teaching of poetry: I
should like to know more about these young people and about
their teachers and the methods of teaching.[5]

This is an interesting case, unlike our other three passages
but not uncommon in expository prose, where the assumed
reader simply has to know who the real author *is* if he is to
understand the message at all. In this instance, he is the late
T. S. Eliot. Implicit in the speaker's words is the knowledge, on the part of both his reader and himself, that he is
speaking for one specific human being, and that the most
distinguished literary figure of his time. How pleasant to meet
Mr. Eliot. This knowledge is modest (or is it smug?) on the
speaker's part, deferential on the reader's part—but it is *there*.
We may imagine messages going out from speaker to assumed
reader something like this:

How pleasant it is for me to acknowledge my academic deficien-
cies when you know exactly who I am! (Besides, *are* they deficien-
cies? You and I know better, don't we?) When I start in to attack
an educational method, my own method can assume the mild
forms of amateurishness, good humor, and mere "spirit of curiosity." My words can be so light because my reputation is so
weighty. You, surely an admirer of my long career, can smile
knowingly when I say that I "should like to know more about"
these teachers and this method. *You* know that I'm going to tear
them apart, but gently, deftly, without losing an ounce of my
urbanity. They are scarcely worth my heavier weapons.

The assumed author of this essay finds that voice very
hard to deny. This is not Tough Talk at all, nor is it exactly
Sweet Talk, nor is it Stuffy. Some readers may find it overly
self-conscious, possibly condescending, possibly banking too
much on the reader's swooning before this great reputation.

But I do not find it so. The spectacle offered here, of the great man unbending, seems to me not unattractive, and I am won more than lost by such carefully human touches as the reference to his income, or the amused use of the slight vulgarism "teenagers." The blunt repetition of "I" and the simple structure of the opening sentences seem candid and there is some deliberately comic hypocrisy in the modest admissions. (I hold no diploma, true, but you know I don't need to!)

We have—or at least I have—a trust in this speaker. Why? Is it because of his overpowering reputation? In large measure, probably. This is a speaker with an enormous advantage, and he takes advantage of his advantage. But it is more than that. The personality that emerges here, with his wit, his urbanity, his refusal to be ruffled, is simply a personality I am willing to go on listening to. The fact that he is about to take a general stand about teaching that is more or less in agreement with all three of our previous voices, and myself, is neither here nor there. The fact that he may also tread on some educational methods I myself espouse (or have been guilty of) is mildly disturbing, but not seriously. It is the character I meet here that makes the difference. He is not pushing me around, like the Tough Talker. He is not cuddling up to me, like the Sweet Talker. He is not holding me off, like the Stuffy Talker. He respects me. I return the compliment.

This is the case of the speaker as famous man. It is, as I say, not uncommon in argumentative prose, though it is seldom so graceful. But it is impossible in fiction, and for most of us it is impossible anyway. You have to be very famous indeed to get away with it. It does show us a respectable voice in operation, but it tells us only a little about how rhetoric can produce a respectable voice without the Real Author looming in the wings. Our questions remain. How are words selected and arranged so that a particular speaking voice is dramatized and identified for us? In the following chapter we shall be looking at two successful introductions, the opening paragraphs of two novels. This look should put us in position to define some characteristics of one particular modern style, one kind of self-dramatization, through a brilliant early example of the Tough Talker. We can then ask how this style is observable in more recent prose, where it has not always been so brilliant.

3

TOUGH TALK
The Rhetoric of Frederic Henry

I did not say anything. I was always embarrassed
by the words . . . .

When a new style swims into our ken, as Hemingway's did
in the 1920s, it is new, or was new, in respect to a historical
situation. People brought to their reading, just as they still do
of course, a set of assumptions about how books ought to be
written. No novelist would be interested in a reader who had
never read a novel, or who had never experienced, as *he* has
experienced, the going literature of the recent past. So Hemingway's assumed reader of the 1920s had an ear tuned to
nineteenth-century rhythms and attitudes; it was in their light
that Hemingway's style appeared so fresh and exciting. It is
still exciting, if not exactly fresh, a generation later, which is
testimony enough to the power of a great writer.

But in order to remind ourselves of some of the stylistic
expectations against which Hemingway was first read, and to
some extent must still be read, it will be useful to contrast the
opening of *A Farewell to Arms* (1929) with the opening of a
standard sort of American novel of forty years earlier. The

opening I have chosen, from W. D. Howells' *A Modern Instance* (1888), has some superficial resemblance in stage setting to Hemingway's opening that may make the contrast in
style the more striking. In each case a narrator is introducing
us to a scene as well as to himself, and both scenes include a
village on a *plain*, in the *summer*, with a view of *mountains*
and a *river*.

PASSAGE A (HOWELLS)

The village stood on a wide plain, and around it rose the mountains. They were green to their tops in summer, and in the winter
white through their serried pines and drifting mists, but at every
season serious and beautiful, furrowed with hollow shadows, and
taking the light on masses and stretches of iron-grey crag. The
river swam through the plain in long curves, and slipped away
at last through an unseen pass to the southward, tracing a score
of miles in its course over a space that measured but three or four.
The plain was very fertile, and its features, if few and of purely
utilitarian beauty, had a rich luxuriance, and there was a tropical
riot of vegetation when the sun of July beat on those northern
fields. They waved with corn and oats to the feet of the mountains, and the potatoes covered a vast acreage with the lines of
their intense, coarse green; the meadows were deep with English
grass to the banks of the river, that, doubling and returning upon
itself, still marked its way with a dense fringe of alders and white
birches.

PASSAGE B (HEMINGWAY)

In the late summer of that year we lived in a house in a village
that looked across the river and the plain to the mountains. In
the bed of the river there were pebbles and boulders, dry and
white in the sun, and the water was clear and swiftly moving and
blue in the channels. Troops went by the house and down the
road and the dust they raised powdered the leaves of the trees.
The trunks of the trees too were dusty and the leaves fell early
that year and we saw the troops marching along the road and the

dust rising and leaves, stirred by the breeze, falling and the soldiers marching and afterward the road bare and white except for the leaves.

The plain was rich with crops; there were many orchards of fruit trees and beyond the plains the mountains were brown and bare. There was fighting in the mountains and at night we could see the flashes from the artillery. In the dark it was like summer lightning, but the nights were cool and there was not the feeling of a storm coming.[1]

Who are these two people talking to us?

The narrator in Passage A (Howells) is concerned with making us see and know the landscape surrounding the village, and he can do this because he can occupy a position where *he* sees and knows this landscape intimately. Let us begin by locating this position, which is expressible in respect to both space and time. Physically, the narrator can speak as from a cloud, a balloon, floating wide-eyed over the plain. He sees large features of the scene—the mountains, the course of the winding river, the fields with their crops. It is a bird's-eye view. He also occupies a favorable position in time. He has been here before, he *knows*. He knows, for example, how the mountains look not only in summer (the *then* of the opening scene), but in winter as well. (Sentence A-2.) He knows (A-3), even though it is not at present visible, that the river slips away "through an unseen pass" to the southward. This is a speaker whose particular rhetorical personality, which would look very strange in a novel of the second half of the twentieth century, serves to inspire our confidence, partly from its very antiquity. Note that as assumed readers we date the speaker immediately, however vaguely, and date ourselves as well, by ruling out some twentieth-century suspicions and expectations. We are introduced to a familiar kind of traditional gentle-manly voice whose tones we associate with Standard Literature, and whose word we accept absolutely. This man knows what there is to know about this scene. We are in good hands.

The man talking in Passage B speaks to us from an utterly different position. As he thinks back on his experience in the village—and note that it is *his* experience that he thinks back on—the positions he occupies are drastically more limited than those of our airborne observer in A. Everything described in B can be seen (or almost seen) from one place, the house where *he* lived. The language keeps reminding us of this limitation by returning to the speaker and his companions (*we*) and their vantage point for seeing and feeling. The house "looked across the river"; "we saw the troops"; "we could see the flashes"; "there was not the feeling of a storm coming." The speaker's range is similarly limited in time; all he tells us about is the way things looked during one particular late summer as it became autumn. The other seasons, before he came to live in the village, or after he left, he presumably doesn't know about. We hear the familiar "flatness" of the voice addressing us, the speaker's refusal to say more than he knows from ordinary human experience. He is close-lipped. The simplicity of his style, the apparent simplicity of it, is of course notorious. You would not call this man genial. He behaves rather as if he had known us, the reader, a long time and therefore doesn't have to pay us very much attention. He is more tense, more intense, than A. And after all, we should observe, he is dealing with images of war, and not with a peaceful New England landscape.

So much for one reader's quick first impression of the two personalities addressing us and the positions from which they speak. But I propose a longer look at some grammatical and rhetorical peculiarities of these two speakers, returning often to their personalities and positions to ask how these have been created, and how we may refine our first impressions. How are these impressions justified by the language, if they are? How do details of wording force us to certain conclusions about the man we're being introduced to? If some of what follows seems alarmingly statistical and detailed, I would argue that only by such devices can we begin to understand the effort that went into these two creative acts.

Words, their size. Everybody knows that Hemingway's diction is characterized by short, simple, largely Anglo-Saxon words. Howells' vocabulary is more conventionally extensive. Actually, in the Howells passage, almost three-quarters of the words are monosyllables, while only one word out of twenty is longer than two syllables. It is hardly an elaborate or affected diction. Yet we recognize in Howells that there are particular words, especially the longer words, which for various reasons would be unthinkable in Hemingway. Among them are *beautiful, utilitarian, luxuriance*—and I shall have more to say about them below. For the present, we note that in passage B, the Hemingway passage, over four-fifths of the words (82 per cent) are of one syllable only, an extremely high proportion. What is more remarkable, only two words, or about one in a hundred, are more than two syllables in length. (These two are *afterward* and *artillery*, neither of them very formidable.) The rigorous selection, or limitation, in vocabulary that these figures imply is drastic, and certainly contributes largely to our sense of a laconic, hard-bitten, close-talking fellow. He is literally *curt*.

Modifiers. An important distinction in the way the two speakers choose words has to do with the frequency of their modifiers. What would we expect of a man who knows, who is magically airborne over the landscape, as against a speaker who is laconically reporting the facts of his own limited experience? We would expect that the former would be more free with his modifiers, would be, that is, willing to name the qualities and virtues of things, not just the things themselves. Actually there are about twice as many modifiers in the Howells as in the Hemingway. Some of Howells' adjectives, in particular, have obvious implications of value: *serious, beautiful, rich, utilitarian.* While many others are simply descriptive (if that is possible), such as *green, deep, dense,* every one of the modifiers in B is of the type that purports to avoid value and simply state facts, especially physical facts: *dry, white, blue, dusty, swiftly,* and so on.

Nouns and repetition. A count of nouns in the two passages results in almost identical figures. But because of a great difference in repetition of nouns, there is a difference in the actual repertoire the two writers use. There are 47 appearances of nouns in A, and because repetition is negligible there are 43 different nouns used. In Hemingway I count 46 noun appearances with a remarkable refrain of repetition. Fourteen nouns appear twice or three times; only 32 different nouns are to be found in the passage. The effect of this rather astonishing contrast is worth speculating on. It helps us, again, to understand why we could call the B narrator "close-lipped." He simply doesn't use many words! There is a critical suggestion to the speaker's personality, as if he were saying, I'm not one of your fancy writers, always scrabbling around for elegant variation. I say what I mean. If I mean the same thing twice, I *say* the same thing twice, and I don't care if it offends the so-called rules of so-called graceful prose.

Imagery, abstract and concrete. It is a commonplace about modern writers, and it may seem to be borne out by our analysis up to this point, that the more recent writers are concerned hardheadedly with things-as-they-are, with precise description rather than with the evaluative blur that we like to think characterizes the older literature. Everybody's passion nowadays for being "concrete" rather than "abstract" represents a fashionable general attitude. But, judging from the present evidence, the commonplace may not be true. Nobody knows, I suspect, how to distinguish concrete words from abstract in any very satisfactory way, but suppose we apply in all innocence this rule of thumb: which of our two speakers tells us more about the scene, supposing we wanted to paint a picture of it? There is no doubt that it is Howells. It is not simply Hemingway's paucity of nouns and modifiers that handicaps him as a scene-painter. It is his very choice of the nouns and modifiers that he does use. Where Hemingway writes *trees*, Howells names them—*alders, birches*. Where Hemingway refers to *crops* and *orchards*, Howells gives us *corn, oats*, and *potatoes*. It is true that Howells includes some words normally thought of as "abstract" (*features, beauty, luxuriance*), while Hemingway gives us plenty of "concrete" nouns, *pebbles* and *boulders, mountains, orchards, soldiers*. But the result is what matters, and in this case the result is that the language creates, in A, a narrator who *cares* about telling us what the landscape looked like, and in B we sense a narrator who cares about something else.

What else does he care about? Why does he, in spite of his superficial and apparent concreteness, tell us so little specifically about the scene? Because the scene, from his position, is not important except as it contributes to his own feelings, his remembered feelings. His recurrences to the act of personal viewing mentioned earlier (*We saw, we could see*) are reminders of the highly personal interest of this speaker. He is not concerned with having us see the landscape, but in having us understand *how he felt*. This is a very different aim;

all his devices of grammar and rhetoric are chosen to achieve this aim.

Sentences, their size and structure. Again the short sentence in Hemingway is a commonplace observation, and it no doubt contributes to the curtness we have been noticing. Actually, in these two passages, the difference is only between an average length of 38 words and of 28 words—nothing very spectacular. Much more interesting is the grammatical structure of the sentences of each passage. In A we have both compound and compound-complex sentences, with considerable subordination of clauses. In B we have largely compound sentences made up of coordinate clauses strung together with *and*. (Sentence B-4 is a good example.) When we count up subordinate clauses in the two passages, we discover that in B there are only two, and they are informal and inconspicuous. "The dust they raised," for instance, gives us a modifying clause without the signal *that*, an omission common in oral speech. We are reminded that the narrator knows us, speaks familiarly, doesn't in fact go out of his way for us much. Modifying clauses in A, on the other hand, are crucially different. Here their formal qualities are directed not toward maintaining a pose of familiarity with a reader, but instead toward seriously clarifying for the reader, whom the speaker has only just met, what the landscape looked like. The second half of Sentence A-5, for example, offers us a subordinate clause of some elegance and considerable skill.

. . . the meadows were deep with English grass to the banks of the river, that, doubling and returning upon itself, still marked its way with a dense fringe of alders and white birches.

One may not wish to go so far as to say that the very phrasing here, in its leisurely meandering, doubles and returns upon itself like the river, but one would have to say, at least, that a subordinate clause of this kind, punctuated in this way, would look very odd in Hemingway. You do not talk this way to someone you know easily and intimately.

More spectacular in the Hemingway style, of course, are the successions of coordinate clauses linked by *and*. It is a highly significant grammatical expression, and its significance can be grasped if one tries irreverently to rewrite a coordinate Hemingway sentence in more traditional patterns of subordination. Here is the original sentence B-4, for instance:

The trunks of the trees too were dusty and the leaves fell early that year and we saw the troops marching along the road and the dust rising and leaves, stirred by the breeze, falling and the soldiers marching and afterward the road bare and white except for the leaves.

Now here is a version attempting to subordinate some of the clauses:

The leaves fell early that year, which revealed the dusty trunks of the trees and the marching troops on the road; when the troops went by, we saw the dust rise, while the leaves fell, stirred by the breeze, but after the soldiers had gone the road was bare and white except for the leaves.

The original B-6 reads this way:

There was fighting in the mountains and at night we could see the flashes from the artillery.

If we subordinate one of these clauses, we must state a relation between them—for example the relation of logical cause:

We knew there was fighting in the mountains, for at night we could see the flashes from the artillery.

Now the damage done to the original, in both cases, is of course catastrophic. In the original B-6, the speaker doesn't say how he knew there was fighting in the mountains. It was just there, ominous, baldly stated. The awareness of the fighting and the seeing of the flashes are all part of a huge complex of personal feeling, and the connections between the various sensations are left (deliberately of course) ambiguous. This is a highly refined example of the leave-it-up-to-the-reader technique that I found so irritating in "Private World" of the preceding chapter.

This is why so many people do not know how to read. They have been taught to turn books into abstractions.

There, as in Hemingway, the logical connection between the two unconnected independent structures was unstated. But there is a difference. In "Private World," the intended connection is plain. What in Hemingway was a suggestive technique for implying several possible connections while stating none, becomes merely a rhetorical gimmick for forcing the reader to supply an obvious meaning. This is what we mean by the Misuse of a Style.

The definite article. I have mentioned a difference in relation with their assumed readers that the two speakers suggest. Whereas the speaker in A keeps his distance, using what we think of as fairly formal discourse, the speaker in B seems to have known the reader before and doesn't trouble himself to explain things as one must for an acquaintance one has just met. A possible cause of this difference between the two speakers can be found in the different ways they use a simple three-letter word—the word *the*. To be statistical again, the incidence of the definite article in the Howells paragraph comes to about 8 per cent; in the Hemingway passage it is about 18 per cent, or almost one word out of every five. It is clearly the Hemingway passage that is unconventional, labeling every other noun with *the*.

What is the effect of such an extraordinary preoccupation?

In the late summer of that year we lived in a house in a village that looked across the river and the plain to the mountains.

One's first naive response to that sentence might be some perfectly pardonable questions. "What year? What river, what plain, what mountains? I don't know what you're talking about." Precisely: the *real* reader doesn't know what the speaker is talking about, but the assumed reader doesn't bother about that. *He* has been placed in a situation where he is expected to assume that he does know what the speaker is talking about. It is as if, for the assumed reader, a conversation had been going on before he opened the book, a conversation that laid the groundwork for all this assumed intimacy. Or it is as if—another analogy—we were suddenly plopped down in a chair listening to a man who has begun telling a story to another man who has just left the room. Curiously the storyteller confuses us with the friend who has just departed, and we find ourselves taking the place of this friend, yoked to the teller as he was. And of course, as always, we can't talk back.

The difference can be realized if again we try an irreverent revision, excising most of the definite articles:

Late in 1915, when I was an officer in the Italian army, my unit lived in a house in a northern Italian village that looked across a river toward some mountains.

In this version, the speaker makes no such assumptions about the common knowledge shared by himself and his assumed reader. Now he names the year and the locale, he defines who "we" are, and his consistent indefinite articles maintain a more distant posture with his reader.[2]

My revision again, naturally, is disastrous. It does more than create distance between reader and speaker. Reading it, one has the impression that the narrator doesn't care much about what he's saying. It starts off like any old war reminiscence. But in Hemingway's version, for many more reasons than I've been able to express here, we feel already the excitement, or what I have to call the intensity, of the narrator. He is deeply involved in his feelings about what he is going to tell us, and perhaps one reason he can give that impression is that he can pretend not to have to worry very much about us, about cueing us in in the conventional way.

The first word of the Howells passage is *The*, but the quickest reading reveals the difference. Here the narrator is describing a scene as if we had never seen it before—as indeed we have not. We need not assume the same kind of intimate relation with the narrator; he keeps us relatively at a distance, and he does not use (as Hemingway does) the first person pronoun. Yet even the Howells narrator launches us somewhat *in medias res*, assuming we will not ask, of his first two words, "What village?" Again the removal of the definite article will show how a speaker can back off even further from his reader, beginning a wholly new relationship with new information: A village stood on a wide plain, and around it rose mountains. One feels, of that sentence, that it should be prefaced by "Once upon a time," and it may be that in telling a fairy story, part of the trick is to assume very little from your reader. Nor is there any effort, in the fairy story, to make the narrator or his tale sound "real." In fact the effort must be just the other way. In the Hemingway kind of story, quite a lot is implied, through intensity of tone, about how seriously, how real, we are to take all this. There is a scale of pretension we could trace, something like this:

Fairy story: Here's a little tale of something that (let's pretend) might have happened a long, long time ago in the Land of Nod.

Howells: Here is a story about people behaving much as people in life do behave; I hope you enjoy it.

Hemingway: This is how it really felt to me when it all happended. (Oh yes, if you insist, it's a *story*.)

My passages can't possibly justify all that. But if there is anything to such a scale, then the Hemingway rhetoric has the effect of including, as part of its fiction, the fiction that all this really happened to a narrator who felt intensely about it, and the reader is maneuvered into a position of sympathy with a person whose principal concern is not with the reader, not with the scene he is describing, but with himself and his own feelings. There is a consequent lift of the voice, a tension in the vocal chords. That is no armchair, relaxed and comfortable, that the Tough Talker occupies.

It will be useful now to summarize the Tough Talker's manner by means of a tentative definition of his personality and rhetoric. In doing so, we remember that our source is only the first 189 words of one Hemingway novel. Nor should we assume that the character described here is absolutely new to literature. What we do have here is an identifiable speaker (Frederic Henry by name), defined in an identifiable rhetoric, some of whose qualities we will be able to recognize in later prose.

A description of a Tough Talker. Frederic Henry is a hard man who has been around in a violent world, and who partially conceals his strong feelings behind a curt manner. He is in fact more concerned with those feelings than he is with the outward scenes he presents, or with cultivating the good wishes of the reader to whom he is introducing himself. He can ignore these traditional services to the reader because he assumes in advance much intimacy and common knowledge. (We are beyond explanations, beyond politenesses.) He presents himself as a believable human character, without omniscience: he knows only what he knows, and is aware of his limitations.

His rhetoric, like his personality, shows its limitations openly: short sentences, "crude" repetitions of words, simple grammatical structures with little subordinating. (I have no use for elegant variation, for the worn-out gentilities of traditional prose.) His tense intimacy with his assumed reader, another man who has been around, is implied by colloquial patterns from oral speech and by a high frequency of the definite article. He lets his reader make logical and other connections between elements. (You know what I mean; I don't have to spell it all out for *you*.) He prefers naming things to describing them, and avoids modification, especially when suggestive of value. All these habits of behavior suggest that he is self-conscious about his language—even about language generally. He is close-lipped, he watches his words.

This suspiciousness about language, only implied in our passage, deserves amplification particularly because it will concern us again later, in other writers. Part of the violent world that the Tough Talker has been around in is the violent verbal world, where words have been so abused that they have lost their lives. In a famous passage later on in *Farewell to Arms* Frederic Henry makes the point explicitly:

I did not say anything. I was always embarrassed by the words sacred, glorious, and sacrifice, and the expression in vain. We had heard them, sometimes standing in the rain almost out of earshot, so that only the shouted words came through, and had read them, on proclamations, now for a long time, and I had seen nothing sacred, and the things that were glorious had no glory and the sacrifices were like the stockyards at Chicago if nothing was done with the meat except to bury it. There were many words that you could not stand to hear and finally only the names of places had dignity. Certain numbers were the same way and certain dates and these with the names of the places were all you could say and have them mean anything. Abstract words such as glory, honor, courage, or hallow were obscene beside the concrete names of villages, and the numbers of roads, the names of rivers, the numbers of regiments and the dates.[3]

Such a negative attitude toward language, however understandable and right in this novel, becomes deadly in later and less skillful hands. For some members of the Beat Generation all language became meaningless—a conviction peculiarly difficult for a writer to live with. The conviction may have had something to do with the poverty of beat style, and with the early demise of that movement. In any event, a self-conscious anxiety about the very reliability of words has become one of the crosses the modern writer has to bear. Fortunately it can be borne in many ways, from comedy to despair.

4

DULLNESS AND DISHONESTY
The Rhetoric of Newswriting

Must a great newspaper be dull?

This chapter considers some examples of how the news of the day is expressed for us, and how, in some of its expressions, a bastard form of the Tough Talker can be detected.

We begin with a conventional sample of "straight" reporting, though concerning events that lend themselves to excitable treatment. Here is a reporter for *The New York Times* (Claude Sitton) beginning his lead article on the race riots in Birmingham, Alabama, in the issue for May 8, 1963.

The police and firemen drove hundreds of rioting Negroes off the streets today with high-pressure hoses and an armored car. The riot broke out after from 2,500 to 3,000 persons rampaged through the business district in two demonstrations and were driven back. The Negroes rained rocks, bottles and brickbats on the law-enforcement officials as they were slowly forced backward by the streams of water. The pressure was so high that the water skinned bark off trees in the parks and along sidewalks. Policemen from surrounding cities and members of the Alabama Highway Patrol rushed to a nine-block area near the business district to help quell the riot. An undetermined number of persons were injured in the demonstrations against segregation. They included the Rev. Fred L. Shuttlesworth, a prominent Negro leader, and two city policemen and a Jefferson County deputy sheriff.

(The National Association for the Advancement of Colored People called for peaceful picketing in 100 cities around the country to protest the actions of the Birmingham officials. In Greenfield Park, N.Y., a group of Conservative rabbis left for Birmingham in a "testimony on behalf of the human rights and dignity" of Negroes.)

I have called this an example of "straight" reporting, and my quotation marks are intended to suggest, of course, that straightness is as absolutely impossible in writing as it is in higher mathematics. Readers of a semantic turn of mind, looking for loaded language in that introduction, might easily challenge some of it. The Negroes "rampaged" through the business district, and "rained" missiles on the police. The sentence about the velocity of the fire hoses would not have been composed by a Southern reporter. But on the whole it is hard to see how the job could have been done much straighter than it has been done here. A little dull, considering the circumstances? Unfeeling? Perhaps a little Stuffy? Or is the horror the more vivid because of the writer's very restraint? At any rate, taking this account as a base of operations, let us look at some alternative ways of reporting that day's events in Birmingham.

At the time when these events took place, the *New York Herald Tribune* was conducting a publicity campaign directed a little desperately at an obvious front-running competitor. MUST A GREAT NEWSPAPER BE DULL?, the billboards were asking, and the answer, in the negative, was presumably to be found in the style of the *Tribune's* own pages. On the same day when the *Times* piece appeared, the *Tribune's* story, under the byline of Charles Portis, began as follows:

Three times during the day, waves of shouting, rock-throwing Negroes had poured into the downtown business district, to be scattered and driven back by battering streams of water from high-pressure hoses and swinging clubs of policemen and highway patrolmen. Now the deserted streets were littered with sodden debris. Here in the shabby streets of the Negro section one of the decisive clashes in the Negro battle against segregation was taking place. Last night a tense quiet settled over the riot-packed city after a day in which both sides altered their battle tactics. The Negro crowds, who for days have hurled themselves against police barriers, divided into small, shifting bands, darted around the police and poured hundreds of separate patrols into the downtown business districts. The police, who had crowded hundreds into the city's jails, abandoned efforts to arrest the demonstrators. They concentrated on herding the mobs toward the 16th Street Baptist Church, headquarters for these unprecedented demonstrations. By day's end, Gov. George Wallace had ordered some 250 state highway patrolmen in to aid beleaguered local police and had warned at an opening session of the Legislature that he would prosecute Negroes for murder if anyone died in the Birmingham riots.

As often, we may begin by asking just where in place and time the two assumed authors are situated. The *Times* man is not, as far as we can tell, anywhere in particular. He is sitting in his hotel room typing out an account of what he has seen or heard during the day just ended. Or he is at a telephone dictating this information to New York. Who knows? Little or no distinction has been made between speaker and assumed author. There is no pretense that the reporter is anywhere else but where, in realistic fact, we assume he *is*, as a working journalist. But the *Tribune* man is far more complex in locating himself. He uses, first, two verb tenses in identifying the time of utterance. During the day waves of Negroes *had poured* (first sentence). When is now? Presumably at the end of the day, at the time of writing. Why, then, *were* littered; why not *are* littered? This particular posture, of using "now" for a time spoken of as already having happened, is common in fiction, where an *imagined* voice can use "now" in that curious and palpably made-up way. The assumed author pretends with one word (now) that he is really there at the moment, while with another word (were) he reminds us that he isn't. Third sentence: *Here* in the shabby streets of the Negro section. Where is here? Where is the speaker? Well, the speaker is apparently in the shabby streets, but the *writer* certainly isn't in the streets. Squatting on the sidewalk with typewriter or telephone? Scarcely. What the writer has done, then, is to invent an imagined speaker, *on the model of the novelist*, who, because he is imaginary, can speak of the situation more authoritatively than any mere hotel-bound reporter. And authoritative this speaker (or, better, narrator) certainly is. It follows, to take a minor example, that he can call the streams from the fire hoses "battering," almost as if he felt them himself. (Compare the *Times* man's sentence about the fire hoses and the bark of trees: evidence he presumably observed personally.) Or, to take a more conspicuous example, it follows that this narrator can label the riot as "one of the decisive clashes in the Negro battle against segregation." How does he know that? He knows it because he is a made-up man, because he is like a teller of a tale, and it is his privilege and his business to know.

Further manifestations of this narrator's free-swinging position can be found in a number of his words and phrases. His willingness to use metaphor (however unoriginally) is characteristic. "Hundreds of rioting Negroes" (*Times*) are "waves" in the *Tribune*. The crowds "hurled themselves" while the police were "herding" the mobs toward the church. Throughout the passage the writer's liberal use of modification is significant. As in our Howells-Hemingway contrast of Chapter

3, we find here a perceptible difference between the two pieces of prose in the number of words used as modifiers—that is, considerably more in the *Tribune* article. And as in Howells, it is the omniscient assumed author who takes the liberty of modifying his nouns with adjectives. Why not? He knows, and can well afford to give us the qualities of things, not just their names. And the difference in genre is of course the whole point: where Howells was writing a clear piece of fiction, the *Tribune* purports to express actual events.

By such language the day's news is transformed into a tale told by a fictitious teller. It may not be dull, but as anyone can see, it can be dangerous. What the *Tribune* writer has done is to impose on a real-life situation an omniscient narrator of the sort familiar to traditional fiction. Must a great newspaper be dull? In this case, at least, the avoidance of "dullness" has been accomplished at the cost of making Birmingham a fictitious place, the kind of place where someone "in charge" (the narrator) can truly know the score. I do not disguise my own moral indignation at this literary make-believe. For Birmingham and its troubles are not fiction; they are serious and complicated matters to be cautiously expressed. Furthermore, insofar as naive readers may not recognize the *Tribune's* fictitiousness, and may assume that this is a Real Birmingham being described, the damage done in the long run to people's minds may be serious.

There is a problem of *genre* here that has attracted some attention just recently. With the publication of Truman Capote's enormously popular *In Cold Blood* (1965), the issue was explicitly raised. Was this factual journalism, or was it fiction? Mr. Capote has made much of his "invention" of a new style, combining the two. The fictional omniscience of his narrating voice is supposed to be justified by years of research, note-taking, tape-recording, and all the industry of the cautious reporter. Nevertheless he feels free to enter the minds of his protagonists and give us their "thoughts." Where are we? This muddle has upset some of his critics, notably Mr. F. W. Dupee, who has complained that Capote is "exploiting the factual authority of journalism and the atmospheric license of fiction."[1]

But the device of the omniscient narrator in news-writing, as an attempt to avoid dullness, has been with us for quite a while. It has been most conspicuous in *Time,* "the weekly news-magazine." The style of *Time* has irked a great many people, and has inspired parodies of considerable venom. *Time's* style has also, obviously, impressed many readers favorably, as the magazine's success over the years must demonstrate. It has not generally been understood that both the outrage and the admiration originate in one pervasive device of style: the intrusion into the news of an omniscient narrator, on the model of works of fiction.

Any random sampling of *Time's* pages will show this omniscient speaker at work. Such a speaker can, for example, know what is going on inside the minds of other people—a privilege open to the fictitious narrator alone.

The cold war, the President felt, was a stalemate. He sensed a deepening international discouragement . . . .

He can *know* the true significance of the events he describes:

To eye and ear, the desultory discussion in the Senate seemed like anything but what it actually was: one of the most . . . .

He can be in possession of the most vivid details concerning events no human could possibly know:

Leaping from his bed one night last January, Dahomey's President Hubert Maga excitedly telephoned military headquarters to report that his residence was being shelled. He soon went back to sleep. As it turned out . . . .

He can temptingly throw out details about a character he is introducing, *as if* the reader already knew whom he was talking about—the suspense-building technique of the story-teller:

They called him "Tawl Tawm." His flamboyant Senate oratory could down an opponent in sweet molasses or hogtie him in barbed wire. He smoked ten 15¢ cigars a day and wore his white hair so long that it crested in curls at the nape of his neck. He dressed . . . .

This piece is not headlined at all—such as "Senator Connolly Dies." Instead it is *titled*—"Tawl Tawm"—in the slightly mysterious way that stories are conventionally titled.[2]

In fact *Time*'s dependence on models of fiction shows up clearly in its headings, where puns and echoes based on actual titles of fiction are common. "Revolution in the Afternoon," "Sounds in the Night," "The Monkey's Pa," are examples from a single issue. These instances of semi-literary semi-sophistication have their bearing on the tone of the magazine, in which the reader is flattered by being in the know with respect to such little jokes. But tricks of title are only a minor weapon in *Time*'s arsenal for putting the reader (fictitiously) in the know. It is the consistent omniscience of the narrating voice that primarily does the job.

How did *Time* describe the events of May 7, 1963, in Birmingham, Alabama? As follows:

The blaze of bombs, the flash of blades, the eerie glow of fire, the keening cries of hatred, the wild dance of terror at night—all this was Birmingham, Alabama.

Birmingham's Negroes had always seemed a docile lot. Downtown at night, they slouched in gloomy huddles beneath street lamps talking softly or not at all. They knew their place: they

were "niggers" in a Jim Crow town, and they bore their degrada-
tion in silence.

But last week they smashed that image forever. The scenes in
Birmingham were unforgettable. There was the Negro youth,
sprawled on his back and spinning across the pavement while
firemen battered him with streams of water so powerful that they
could strip the bark off trees. There was the Negro woman, pinned
to the ground by cops, one of them with his knee dug into her
throat. There was the white man who watched hymn-singing
Negroes burst from a sweltering church and growled: "We ought
to shoot every damned one of them." And there was the little
Negro girl, splendid in a newly starched dress, who marched out
of a church, looked toward a massed line of pistol-packing cops,
and called to a laggard friend: "Hurry up, Lucile. If you stay
behind you won't get arrested with our group."

The postures of Knowing taken here are obvious enough
and hardly need stressing. "All this was Birmingham." The
narrator knows the past, for the Negroes "had always seemed"
docile. He has seen them "in gloomy huddles" over a long
period of time; this concrete description implies close personal
knowledge. They knew their place, he says, echoing ironically
the white man's cliché, of which again he seems to have an
intimate knowledge. "But last week they smashed that image
forever": now he knows the future too. Is that the news? Or is
it the kind of statement an all-knowing story-teller can make
about a place he has invented? (Of course we have to say, for
this writer, that subsequent events have justified some of his
fictitious wisdom!)

The suspicion is tempting that the *real* author of this piece
never left his air-conditioned office in Manhattan's Time-Life
Building. What he may have done was to read a lot of other
people's accounts of Birmingham, including the *Times* man's
observation about fire hoses and tree bark, which he then
paraphrased in the manner of the novelist. More accurately, I

suppose, this prose is the work of several hands, one or two of whom may actually have been on the scene in Birmingham.

But omniscience is not the only thing to notice about this narrator's use of words. The reader who reacts to that barrage of definite articles in *Time*'s first sentence may be reminded of an old friend.

The blaze of bombs, the flash of blades, the eerie glow of fire, the keening cries of hatred, the wild dance of terror . . . .

Part of the speaker's relation with the reader is that of a shared knowledgeable awareness of just the sort of "blaze" and "flash" and "eerie glow" the speaker is talking about. *You* know what I mean. It is the familiar intimacy of the Tough Talker, who implies that he already knows his reader before the story opens.

Actually, once the first sentence is over with, the writer for *Time* uses somewhat fewer definite articles than the writers of our other two Birmingham passages. But he has additional rhetorical characteristics that, statistically at least, carry him much closer to Frederic Henry than is the case with the other two. Most important is the sheer size of his words. A count of monosyllables in all three passages shows that whereas in the *Times* and *Tribune* a little over half of the words are of one syllable, over three-quarters of *Time*'s diction is monosyllabic. In a count of longer words, those of three syllables or more, the *Times* piece shows 15 per cent, the *Tribune* 12 per cent, and *Time* only 5 per cent. And even these are simple and repetitious; "Birmingham" appears three times. We recall that the Tough Talker is chary with modification. If we list the words in each passage being used to modify nouns (omitting articles and demonstrative and personal pronouns), we discover that the *Time* writer, for all his eerie glows and keening

cries, has the least modification of the three, while the *Tribune*
piece has the most.

A chart of such information may be useful:

	Times	Tribune	Time
Total words in passage	193	201	214
Average sentence length	22	25	19
Monosyllables (% of total words)	55%	57%	78%
Longer words (3 syllables & over)	15%	12%	5%
Modifiers of nouns	15%	19%	11%

Do such figures prove anything? Probably not by themselves, unless we can feel, in the tone of the *Time* passage,
that particular intensity and intimacy we noted in the introduction to *Farewell to Arms*. Can we? For all the embarrassing
bad writing in the *Time* passage, I hope it is clear that we can.
The speaker, surely "a hard man who has been around in a
violent world," expects of us intimacy of a special closeness.
If we are to become the sympathetic assumed reader of these
words (which I personally find most difficult), we share a
world defined in tight-lipped simplicity of language. It is a
world where policemen are always cops and violence is taken
for granted, and where crude pathos (the little Negro girl at
the end) is expected to move us deeply right through the
toughness. Beneath that harsh voice (as often, even in Hemingway) there beats all too visibly a heart of sugar. In fact
the triteness of the piece is such as to give us momentary
pause about our whole response so far. Can this very triteness
be intended? Those piled-up alliterative clichés at the start—
the blaze of bombs, the keening cries—suggest possibly an
even further intimacy with the reader that may conceivably
run something like this: You and I know this is mostly a
verbal game. You recognize as I do the familiar theatrical
phrases from who-done-it literature with which I adorn this

account, and you recognize that I'm not trying to *tell you* anything about Birmingham. I'm just wittily entertaining you for a few moments after a busy day. After all, you've already read last week's newspapers. This is decorative.

If there is anything to the suspicions I have just uttered (and I am truly doubtful), then Timestyle has to be seen as cynical in the extreme. For if, as seems remotely possible, the sophisticated reader is to see this writer's pose as after all not tough and intense, but mock-tough, then the two of them, reader and writer, are engaged in a most irresponsible game. These are not events to play games with. The real trouble is that I, as a reader, can't tell whether this is a game or not.

And if it is not, then we return to locate again one huge distinction between the Tough Talker we saw in Hemingway and the one we see here. It is true that some of the Tough Talker's rhetoric is here visible: short sentences, simplified diction, relatively low modification. But omniscience has been added! We have an intense, human-sounding, tough-talking narrator *without* any human limitations. He knows. When, in other words, you invent a voice that asserts deep and violent feeling, and close intimacy with the reader, and omniscience, you have a public address system of formidable power. And when you apply that voice to the "reporting" of the *news*, you have committed an act of intellectual dishonesty.

In this comparison of three expressions of the news, the restraint of *The New York Times* has seemed to come off with highest marks. But let not the *Times* relax its vigil. The fact is that the charms of fiction-writing have beguiled the *Times* writers too, though usually without the rhetoric of the Tough Talker. We can see fictitious omniscience expecially in the Sunday supplement called "The News of the Week in Review," where, in summarizing the week's news, it is apparently tempting to talk as if one knew what happened.

THE COUP

The time was just before 3 A.M. in Washington on Friday. In the "situation room" in the White House basement, a command center which receives diplomatic and intelligence reports from around the world, a message from the U. S. Embassy in Saigon clattered off one of the teletype machines. A watch officer phoned . . . .

Without belaboring the point one can certainly make out in these lines the suspenseful devices of the novelist, from the mysterious title and *in-medias-res* beginning to the teletype machine that clattered off a message. Who heard it clatter? This is a case of the *Times* man having read his *Time* too well and too often rather than the other way around.

One appreciates any effort by journalists to make the reading of the news less of a chore and a bore. Nobody wants to be dull. But if the alternative to dullness is dishonesty, it may be better to be dull. On the other hand there are surely other alternatives. Without trying to tell the newswriter his business, I should suppose that a concrete and sober account of what a reporter *did* during his day's work would be, in many cases, neither dull nor dishonest. Such an account would not, to be sure, leave us with the satisfied feeling of knowing the Real Scoop on Birmingham, or the White House, or the Wide World. But as I have already said too often, this is not a feeling to be encouraged anyway.

5

FREE-STYLE
The Rhetoric of Unreliable Narrators

I don't mean to be ironic . . . .

An interest in "point-of-view problems" has characterized literary people increasingly in recent years. Their interest may reflect the importance placed on methods of observation, the relativism of the observer's eye, by modern scientists, historians, and intellectuals generally. That creative literary artists themselves share the interest can be demonstrated by a look at mid-twentieth-century fiction. Modern novelists, perhaps as never before, have been projecting first-person-singular narrators who tell their own stories, or heroes whose limited viewpoints dominate the perceptions of the narrator. Personalities and attitudes revealed through limitations in point of view make up a good part of the reader's interest in the story. To mention a distinguished early example, Faulkner in such a book as *As I Lay Dying* presents situations described in sequence by a number of characters, in sometimes conflicting reports, without the assistance of any conventional narrator at all. You decide which ones to believe. (This is the Tough Talker's refusal to subordinate parts of a sentence, translated into larger terms.) Similarly, in England, Joyce Cary has written whole trilogies in which the action is to be understood (if that is the word) only after we have experienced all the varying expressions of it by the different "I" narrators of the different volumes. It is fast becoming a convention in novels to use as chapter headings the name of a single character, whose unique position will be dramatized in the chapter. A fine example is Wright Morris' *Ceremony in Lone Tree*, 1960.

This increasing consciousness, on the part of the authors, of their performances as role-players has had its effect on the Tough Talker. What has happened to the Tough Talker, in much serious fiction since Hemingway, is that we have lost confidence in him for the good reason that his assumed author seems so very aware that it's all just a performance. The assumed author standing behind his narrator stands nowhere nearly so *squarely* behind him as Hemingway's assumed author behind Frederic Henry. In fact the precise relation between narrator-hero and assumed author has become exceedingly difficult to assess, as the reader himself senses the assumed author's reservations about the hero's language. The very Tough Talk itself seems satirized, or almost satirized, or possibly satirized. The result is that the whole reading experience, while gaining in ambiguity and a kind of sophistication, has been weakened in force and directness. The Tough Talker has lost his punch.

Or to put it another way: in defining the Hemingway brand of Tough Talker, I stressed his human limitations, his reality as another man like ourselves, who says only what he *can* say. And I mentioned his suspicions of language, especially in traditional expression. These qualities of the Tough

Talker's character have become exaggerated by recent writers of fiction—until the narrator becomes so human, so limited, so much "just like us" that we wonder how much we are expected to see right through him. Often, as I shall try to show, we may wonder in vain.

In this respect the novelist has taken a precisely different route from the journalist's: whereas the novelist exaggerates the human limitations, the journalist, as we saw, has added omniscience to the Tough Talker's rhetoric.

Before examining some evidence for these changes, though, we remind ourselves that the first-person-singular narrator telling his own story has a long and distinguished history, and in some works of the past he has been clothed with enough complexity and self-consciousness to please almost anybody. (Sterne's Tristram Shandy is an example.) Simpler creations, in which a fictitious narrator-hero straightforwardly relates the story of his life, have produced some of literature's most venerable monuments. Once again, preparing to taste the full flavor of our own time, let us recall a narrating voice from the good gray nineteenth century. Here is David Copperfield introducing himself:

Whether I shall turn out to be the hero of my own life, or whether that station will be held by anybody else, these pages must show. To begin my life with the beginning of my life, I record that I was born (as I have been informed and believe) on a Friday, at twelve o'clock at night. It was remarked that the clock began to strike, and I began to cry, simultaneously.

In consideration of the day and hour of my birth, it was declared by the nurse and by some sage women in the neighborhood who had taken a lively interest in me several months before there was any possibility of our becoming personally acquainted, first that I was destined to be unlucky in life; and secondly, that I was

privileged to see ghosts and spirits: both these gifts inevitably
attaching, as they believed, to all unlucky infants of either gender
born toward the small hours on a Friday night.

How pleasant it is to pause for a moment with that genial
and civilized narrator. Once again (as in Howells) we know
we are in good hands. In response to obvious cues, we set our
expectations in certain restricted but secure directions: we
too become a person like this well-behaved and good-humored
fellow who so unhurriedly begins the story of his life. The
easy word-play in his phrasing—to begin my life with the beginning of my life—is not earth-shaking, but we want no more.
The ominous note in the second paragraph is struck shortly,
the speaker appearing to take little stock in those dire predic-
tions of ill fortune. But the irony of "sage women," though
clear, is not hostile, and the ominous note remains, however
subtle. The speaker is above all unexcited and detached, as
his repeated mild humor reminds us, and we settle back comfortably in rapport with the sympathetic assumed author
behind him.

His rhetoric, of course, supports his personality; his rhetoric
is his personality. His longer words, even when used semi-
humorously, as in "inevitably attaching," promote our awareness of his urbanity and maturity. (He has fewer monosyllables than Howells, and three times as many longer words,
of three syllables or more.) His sentences, averaging some
forty words each, are organized in a most orderly fashion, with
much dependence on parallel structures, some of them rather
elaborate. Whether I shall turn out to be the hero . . . or
whether that station will be held by anybody else. The clock
began to strike, and I began to cry. First that I was destined
. . . and secondly, that I was privileged . . .: both these gifts,
and so on. The frequent passive verbs are suggestive, sup-

porting the unexcited detachment I have mentioned, even though it's himself he is detached from. It was all a long time ago, over and done with. No cause for alarm.

Now, with the familiar gentlemanly sounds of Mr. Copperfield ringing in the ear, let us try this introduction from another autobiography in fiction, composed just about a century later and rapidly becoming almost as familiar:

> I am an American, Chicago born—Chicago, that somber city—and go at things as I have taught myself, free-style, and will make the record in my own way: first to knock, first admitted; sometimes an innocent knock, sometimes a not so innocent. But a man's character is his fate, says Heraclitus, and in the end there isn't any way to disguise the nature of the knocks by acoustical work on the door or by gloving the knuckles.
> Everybody knows there is no fineness or accuracy in suppression; if you hold down one thing you hold down the adjoining.
> My own parents were not much to me, though I cared for my mother. She was simple-minded, and what I learned from her was not what she taught, but on the order of object lessons. She didn't have much to teach, poor woman.[1]

A reader brought up entirely on Dickensian tones of voice (if we can imagine such a one) might be forgiven for responding to that introduction with incredulity. Why, this man is crazy! And we should not, I think, utterly dismiss such a response in ourselves, however much we may be accustomed to wild and woolly modern prose. The craziness is part of the act, and Saul Bellow would be properly discouraged, I suspect, if a reader were to accept Augie March as just one more voice of an ordinary common-sense sort. "I record that I was born (as I have been informed and believe)," easily says David Copperfield, and we too believe, having as little cause for doubt as he. The process of recording becomes something quite different as undertaken by Augie, who "will make the record in my own way." *Free-style* is his term. First to knock, first admitted. There is going to be no effort to organize this life in long, orderly sentences made up of parallel structures. No suppression. Let it come.

And come it does: Chicago and Heraclitus, acoustical work on the door and gloving the knuckles, learned lingo and informal contractions. Is this our old friend the Tough Talker? If we limit ourselves simply to our first impressionistic definition—"a hard man who has been around"—then Augie probably qualifies. And some of his rhetoric, if examined statistically and in relation to Copperfield's, looks indeed tough. Augie's sentences are half as long as David Copperfield's, his monosyllables are a little more frequent, his longer words a little less frequent, and his subordinate clauses are a fraction of the other's. Augie has none of the detachment from reader and self that Copperfield's elaborate sentences and passive verbs suggested. Instead, there is considerable intimacy in the colloquial language, while the free-style mannerisms at the same time tell us that Augie isn't really bothering about us very much. He is self-absorbed, like Frederic Henry; he will make the record in his own way, and you and I had better stay with it as best we can.

But Augie, for all he is a Tough Talker, is curiously unsure of himself. Part of the unsureness can be found in the juxtaposition I have mentioned, of learned and lowbrow diction. Augie is a kind of innocent: he has been around all right, but there are some things he seems not to know, things we *do* know. (I say "seems" because there is room for doubt, as we shall see.) One of the things Augie seems not to know is that you don't usually talk about Heraclitus, acoustical work, and gloving the knuckles in the same breath. Or if you do, you indicate somehow that you're aware this is curious verbal behavior. Is it a joke? Yes. Is Augie in on the joke? Probably? Maybe? Is there doubt about this? Yes. For me, this is not the only cause for doubt in the passage. Yet before going on, I should say, speaking personally as a reader, that even though I do not feel "in good hands," in the Dickens-Howells sense, the hands I do feel in are marvelously exciting, entertaining, and stimulating. The abrupt changes in tone may be bewildering, but they are spectacular. Wisdom from the Greeks is followed by the informality of "there isn't any way." The polysyllables of "no fineness or accuracy in suppression" are followed by the conversational "if you hold down one thing, you hold down the adjoining." But does Augie know what he's doing? I am not sure. Does Bellow? The whole metaphor of knocks on the door seems dragged out to ludicrous lengths. Does Augie think they're ludicrous, or is it just me and the assumed author? (Or is it just me?) When he tells us a moment later that his mother was simple-minded, an unfriendly reader might well surmise that Augie comes by his thought-processes honestly.

But Augie, of course, is no idiot. As the rest of this huge novel makes plain, Augie is a bright, resourceful, thoughtful, poverty-stricken, opportunistic, self-educated young man raised on the seamy side of Chicago and it may be that this mixed background can make his mixed way of talk plausible. The hint of innocence we see in these opening lines continues in the book. But my problem also persists. Since the assumed author never speaks in his own voice, how much are we to consider Augie's an attractive wide-eyed approach to life and how much are we to consider it limited, amusing, or plain wrong? And if you answer that question by saying that it's every reader for himself, then you define the novel in our time in terms radically different from the whole history of literature.

Take another example. Augie says, in his third sentence, giving it a paragraph all to itself:

Everybody knows there is no fineness or accuracy in suppression; if you hold down one thing you hold down the adjoining.

Now my question becomes: am I to take this statement as expressing his limitations? The question is important, for it concerns how I am going to take what Augie goes on to tell me. What is the message that I am receiving from the assumed author? Is it this?

Augie's statement is absolutely right: you and I know too that all suppression is bad. Everybody knows that.

Or is it this?

You and I know that this statement is over-simple, maybe even mistaken, but it's the sort of thing our friend Augie *would* say, isn't it. Don't expect any intellectual reservations from Augie; let freedom ring. Augie is, as you see, an attractive fellow, but you'd better have your grain of salt handy when he sounds off like this.

In my eagerness to like and admire this novel, I am assuming my message from the assumed author to be more like the second than the first. Augie's muddle of free-style talk helps me to decide. But I am not entirely happy nevertheless. For like most Tough Talkers, this voice seems to speak with strength and sincerity, as if we were expected to admire and agree almost without reservation. His very refusal to play the game of genteel literary tradition is part of his strength, part of what apparently seeks to persuade me to take him seriously. He feels, he suffers. Am I not to feel and suffer too? But can I feel and suffer with a fellow who sometimes talks foolishly? Yes, of course I can: witness Huck Finn. But if I am to do this, I must know where the assumed author is standing, for otherwise I may find myself suspecting that the assumed author is talking foolishly, and this is disastrous. There can be no feeling or suffering where that suspicion is a possibility.

By far the most thoroughgoing study of questions like these is that written by Wayne Booth, in his influential *The Rhetoric of Fiction* (1961). Mr. Booth's argument is that modern novelists have been "getting away with murder" by producing "unreliable" narrators for whom their creators take no responsibility. That's not me talking, that's just my hero. Such a rebuttal by the author sounds plausible: David Copperfield is not Dickens; Huck Finn is not Clemens. But there is a crucial difference. In both *David Copperfield* and *Huck,* we know precisely the attitude we are expected to take toward the hero, because we are aware of a clearly defined assumed author in the background. In the case of Augie March, we have no such reliance. And in varying degrees we have the same difficulty with many of Augie's contemporaries in fiction. It is all very lifelike, this of not knowing whether to laugh *at* or *with* one's new acquaintance. It happens every day. But is art daily life? The serious question is raised whether confusions like this are possible in what we think of as Good Literature. Or if they are, then our concept of what Good Literature is must be redefined drastically. How much disorder are you prepared to stand; how close to the heart of the work can disorder be permitted to penetrate?[2]

A related development in the character of the Tough Talker, as he has matured since Hemingway, is that, like Augie,

he has picked up an education. Or, more accurately—for
Frederic Henry was educated too—he now displays his education. He has read Heraclitus. Curiously, this show of learning,
intellectual sophistication, and wit, while it adds wonderful resources for entertainment, intensifies the ambiguity
rather than reducing it. The Tough Talk remains, spare, colloquial, "simple-minded," interlaced with the learning, and
the two can cancel each other's force. The Tough Talker's
power can be undermined when it is presented with built-in
ironies, or possible ironies. When the ironies may be directed
against the very toughness of the talker's talk, the possibilities
for confusion are immense. The assumed author may be so
far in the background, protected by so many subtle reservations about his own hero's words, that he becomes incom-
municado.

The "perfect" narrator-hero Tough Talker of our time is a
man who can master both lowbrow and highbrow language,
and he uses either to cast ironical doubt on the other. Naturally, his diction and rhetoric differ somewhat from the Hemingway Tough Talker, though they share many qualities of
style. He can be a self-educated alumnus of the slums, like
Augie. Or he can be a formally educated or even aristocratic
fellow who has repudiated his advantages to experience the
hard knocks of the vulgar world. Such a one, possibly an important early example of the development I am describing, is
Jack Burden, narrator of *All the King's Men* (1946). Jack
was a graduate student in history who walked out before taking his doctor's degree; he knows a lot about everything. Much
of the novel is taken up with a lengthy subplot out of Jack's
historical researches. It suits Robert Penn Warren's purpose
that his narrator should comment richly and sensitively from
time to time on the action, complete with learned and literary

references, and this Jack is equipped to do. He is a refined sensibility. But Jack is also an ex-newspaper reporter, a hard guy, a loyal assistant to a political dictator. Here is the way he begins his story:

> To get there you follow Highway 58, going northeast out of the city, and it is a good highway and new. Or was new, that day we went up it. You look up the highway and it is straight for miles, coming at you, with the black line down the center coming at and at you, black and silk and tarry-shining against the white of the slab, and the heat dazzles up from the white slab so that only the black line is clear, coming at you with the whine of the tires, and if you don't quit staring at that line and don't take a few deep breaths and slap yourself hard on the back of the neck you'll hypnotize yourself and you'll come to just at the moment when the right front wheel hooks over into the black dirt shoulder off the slab, and you'll try to jerk her back on but you can't because the slab is high like a curb, and maybe you'll try to reach to turn off the ignition just as she starts the dive. But you won't make it, of course.[3]

The exciting rhetoric here is in several ways close to the rhetoric of Frederic Henry—except of course for the length of that endless sentence, which in itself, cheek by jowl with tiny sentences, thumbs its nose at the proprieties of genteel prose. The proportion of monosyllables is even higher than Hemingway's (86 per cent), and this may be about as far as you can go without sounding like baby-talk. (Or does it sound like baby-talk already?) The words of more than two syllables number exactly four: *58, tarry-shining, hypnotize, ignition.* There is a high incidence of the definite article (over 10 per cent). There is the characteristic repetition: over half the words we read in this passage we read for the second, third, or fourth time. And the intimacy with the reader is reinforced not only by the repeated "you" (13 times), instead of "one," but also by the dramatically mysterious opening sentence. "To get there you follow Highway 58, going northeast out of the city. . . ." Where is there? What city? It is assumed we know.

What are we to think of a graduate student in history and a sensitive soul who talks to us this way? What does the assumed author think of this manner of expression? If that endless sentence seems affected to us, if the repetition of simple words looks artificial, what then? Is our quarrel with Jack Burden, a mixed-up young man, carefully contrived by his creator to display just these weaknesses? Is Jack ironically aware of his own tough-talking excesses? Or is our quarrel with the assumed author himself, who just possibly has not made up his mind who Jack is? If the latter, the effect is serious. Mr. Warren, in my view a magnificent writer, has written and re-written this story several times, in several forms, and in some versions (for the stage) the figure of Jack Burden has almost disappeared, while the story has centered on Willie Stark, the dictator-politician. No doubt there are good reasons for such reemphasis; one of them might be a continuing uneasiness about how to "handle" Jack Burden.[4]

Or try another, more recent example of a new Tough Talker, one who wears his sophistication more obviously from the start, who is generally more lighthearted if not frivolous, but whose assumed author presents similar difficulties of clear definition.

My story begins, like everything else, on the beach. Beaches are the same the world over, you peel down, then you peel off; they serve you up raw meat, or flesh nicely basted in olive oil. A strip of sun and sand where the sex is alert, the mind is numb. The beach in question, one of the best, is near where Sunset Boulevard meets the sea. I don't mean to be ironic. California is that way naturally. It's hard to do malice to California, but this particular strip might have been in Acapulco, or down in Rio, or along the Riviera. If it's world brotherhood you want, go to the beach. If you like parallels, the beach is where we came in, and where we'll go out. Having crawled from the sea, we're now crawling back to it. That solution of salt in the blood is calling us home. And in a mammary age, what better place to compensate for an unsuckled childhood?[5]

There is no need to pester to death this delightful narrator (whose name is Earl Horter). He is, to be sure, a fairly hard man and he has been around all right, though the world he has been around in is scarcely as violent as Frederic Henry's. The toughness of his character is additionally sweetened by the fact that he is less self-centered, more polite than the Hemingway narrator. He knows we exist, even if his approach to us is impersonal and flip. "If it's world brotherhood you want, go to the beach." I don't suppose we *do* want world brotherhood, if he puts it that way, but after what we've been through, it's nice of Earl to mention us at all.

There are, however, some problems. "The beach in question, one of the best. . . ." Here "best" means a place where the sex is especially alert, the mind especially numb. Fine, as long as one is certain that Earl too knows this is a pretty funny definition of "best." He does, no doubt, but I sympathize with anyone who might suspect otherwise and suffer confusion therefore. Earl is obviously a terribly bright fellow, as smart as Augie and Jack Burden, but on the other hand he does seem to be spending a lot of time on the beach, pursuing just those pleasures he so cleverly makes fun of. Do we therefore detach ourselves from complete sympathy with him, recognizing in the assumed author a superior being who, with us, sees our friend's weaknesses and smart talk? Is our hero really smart, or just vulgar smart?

"That solution of salt in the blood is calling us home." Is
that real serious Wit, shared by narrator and assumed author
alike? No. Is it then a sort of joke wit, making delicate mock-
ery of pretentious literary ways of talk, and uttered in a spirit
of high jinks felt by the narrator and assumed author in
common? Probably. Or is it a joke that the narrator thinks is
truly clever, but that the assumed author (and you and I)
know to be at best smart-fashionable? Possibly. I am very
much amused by this fellow, but I am genuinely unsure
whether my amusement is shared by him, in just my way.
And let no one presume that these are trivial questions. They
affect the way I am expected to take the whole book.

One thing we can say for certain about Earl: he is self-
conscious about language, almost to the point of being apolo-
getic. "I don't mean to be ironic." "If you like parallels." The
nervousness about words that we pointed out in Hemingway's
Tough Talker has become by this time an overt attentiveness
to rhetoric, including even the terminology of rhetoric. In
more serious, or more ambitious, literature, such preoccupation may lead to confessions almost ludicrous. We have fictitious narrators explicit aware of their awesome responsibilities, and telling us all about them, even to the point of
assuming the fiction of becoming still somebody else. My
example is from J. D. Salinger's "Zooey," which begins with
almost four pages of "author's formal introduction." The following are excerpts:

. . . We begin with that ever fresh and exciting odium: the
author's formal introduction. The one I have in mind not only
is wordy and earnest beyond my wildest dreams, but is, to boot,
rather excruciatingly personal. . . . . To get straight to the worst,
what I'm about to offer isn't really a short story at all but a sort
of prose home movie . . . . In just a moment, the youngest Glass
boy will be seen reading an exceedingly lengthy letter (which

will be reprinted here *in full*, I can safely promise) sent to him by his eldest living brother, Buddy Glass. The style of the letter, I'm told, bears a considerably more than passing resemblance to the style, or written mannerisms, of this narrator, and the general reader will no doubt jump to the heady conclusion that the writer of the letter and I are one and the same person. Jump he will, and, I'm afraid, jump he should. We will, however, leave this Buddy Glass in the third person from here on in. At least, I see no good reason to take him out of it.[6]

This is surely curious, the rhetoric of the rhetorician, complete with terms: *author's introduction, wordy, prose, style, written mannerisms, third person, narrator, writer, narrator* again. The relation between this self-absorbed fellow and his assumed author, also a rhetorical character no doubt, is baffling, and distracting. Insofar as we suspect a close identity between the voice of author and narrator ("jump he should"), we are, or at least I am, simply irritated. Why doesn't he stop messing around and tell his darn story? The legitimate anxiety about language manifested by the Tough Talker has become an absorption in the subject, at least for several pages, and it is certainly a Sign of the Times that such self-absorption should be tolerated in, of all things, a best-seller.[7]

Another recent though less popular novel is equally explicit in confessing to the reader the complications of self-dramatization. In Hayden Carruth's *Appendix A* (1963), the "narrator" (whose mysterious identity certainly deserves the quotation marks) tells us in so many words that he may be writing a "novel or autobiography or dissertation or whatever the hell it is—I haven't really decided yet." And he appeals directly for the reader's sympathy in language that is more Sweet than it is Tough:

The main thing is, I wanted to establish friendly relations right here at the beginning of this novel or autobiography or dissertation or whatever the hell it is—I haven't really decided yet. I'm going to be relying on you a good deal from now on, you see: for patience and understanding and all that; and so I thought I'd best start right out by addressing you directly, though of course I realize it's an unusual way to begin a book. But it isn't the same as sticking my foot in your door, is it? I hope not; I've no desire to be unmannerly or overbearing—not like some of the young guys writing nowadays. You can always shut me out any time you want to, just by closing the book.[8]

Such unbuttoned friendliness, such nervous anxiety to please, is a far cry from Frederic Henry's hard-headed refusal to hold hands with us. Tip it just a little and it is the approach of the advertising copy-writer, to be examined in our next chapter. But there is this great difference: it is *not* an ad, no heading at the top of the page announces "Advertisement," no luscious illustration decorates the prose. This is a novel. The question is, do we laugh at this person for his self-consciousness? Surely we are not expected to "take" his Sweet Talk as he seems to intend it. Or are we? Is there an author's second self who knows better? This is a wavering tone, semi-semi-ironic, in which the author's own involvement in his narrator, plus his own awareness of that narrator's shortcomings, has produced a style to which it is exceedingly difficult to respond.

What all this comes down to is a curious confession on the part of the author-narrator. It is: I know I'm vulgar (and you must forgive me) but I *know* I'm vulgar (and you must admire my self-awareness). This is a very tricky posture to maintain without falling over one way or the other. The attempt to maintain it is, I conclude, a central problem of modern prose style in fiction.

6

SWEET TALK
The Rhetoric of Advertising

More beef than you'd ever expect in a sauce.

Among the various short introductions we have so far considered, there are six that have seemed to qualify, in their different ways, as Tough Talk. That is, each of them has put forward a version of "a hard man who has been around," a man who implies an intimate relation with his reader, but who often at the same time seems preoccupied with his own view of experience almost to the exclusion of the reader. (The phrase "private eye" may be singularly apt.) As we have already hinted, and as we shall see later in more detail, these six characters share specific qualities of style, in word-choice and arrangement, that set them apart from other voices we have been listening to.

Our six Tough Talkers were these:

1. "Private World" (*Saturday Review* essay on teaching), Chapter 2;
2. Frederic Henry (*Farewell to Arms*), Chapter 3;
3. *Time* (report on Birmingham riots), Chapter 4;

71

4. Augie March (*Adventures of*), Chapter 5;
5. Jack Burden (*All the King's Men*), Chapter 5;
6. Earl Horter (*Love among the Cannibals*), Chapter 5.

Any similar six or sixty would do as well. These happen to be the Tough Talkers I am considering here. Lumped together, the six make up a tiny sampling of Toughness—a little over a thousand words. A summary of the qualities of language they share can begin to define the style of Tough Talk, though naturally the definition is tentative in the extreme. For example, of vocabulary one can at least say the obvious: that our Tough Talkers mostly use more one-syllable words and fewer longer words than the other voices we have quoted. In a random way, we have observed such characteristics in the styles of Toughness as a high frequency of the determiner *the*, relatively few modifiers, simple subordinate clauses. In this chapter I ask how the language of advertising may be compared with what we have called Tough Talk. If clear differences in style can be identified, what are they?

More than one observer has remarked that the freshest writing going on nowadays comes from the ad agencies on Madison Avenue. If there is anything to that, we should be able to say what's fresh about it, and what kinds of voice are produced by such freshness. More, we should be able, by comparing details of Madison Avenue style with those of Tough Talk, to indicate some rhetorical techniques by which the adwriter characteristically makes his devastating pitch.

The first thing to do is look at some ads. I offer eight of them below—that is, I reproduce the first hundred words or so (often the whole) of eight ads plucked out of magazines. I make no apology for the arbitrary choice: these simply seemed to me interesting rhetorically. First to knock, first admitted. They offer a grabbag of goods and services: a bank, a magazine, a whisky, a telephone gadget, a bath soap, a prepared dinner, a refrigerator, and a car. But you needn't buy a thing to enjoy the rhetoric, and no salesman will call.

For convenience I label this chunk of language Advertising Rhetoric of Madison Avenue, or AROMA for short.

AD #1

For a better way to take care of your nest egg, talk to the people at Chase Manhattan. So many otherwise well-ordered people unaccountably lose their touch when the subject is personal investments.

If you're letting investment cares compete with the quiet hours —don't. Get hold of The Chase Manhattan Bank's Personal Trust Division right away and let it take over.

And, if you're interested, the Personal Trust Division will also go out of its way to act as your Executor and Trustee, advise you on your estate with you and your lawyer.

AD #2

People listen to people who *know*. Years ago Newsweek broke the language barrier by publishing straight facts in plain English. The effect on communications was startling. Today, more people know what they're talking about. And because these people have made up their own minds, they can communicate more meaningfully to other people. Advertisers are aware of this communications chain-of-command. They have found that through Newsweek it also moves goods. We can elaborate on this subject with all sorts of compelling statistics. But we'd much rather try it first in plain English: More *news*—more *straight news*—in NEWSWEEK.

AD #3

You can't tell one scotch from another. Or can you? Identifying a scotch is a rare skill confined to the rarefied and mysterious world of the connoisseur. The layman, however, is content with his limited but perfectly adequate ability to know what he likes. (Every man his own connoisseur.) It happens that out of the many brands of scotch available most people choose Johnnie Walker—the Scotch of Scotch. They have made it the world's best-selling scotch. It is specially and delightfully different. Different in a way that most people prefer.

AD #4

They're all on the telephone!
It's the new Bell Speakerphone. It's a hands-free, group-talk, across-the-room kind of telephone. About as flexible as a phone can be. Perfect for "conference" conversations. Ideal when you need both hands free for writing or filing or searching. Just right when it's more convenient for you to talk from another part of the room.

Of course, you can regulate volume, move the microphone or speaker anywhere on your desk or a table, switch to the handset for privacy, or use it for intercom calls. Think of the people on your staff who can benefit from this versatile new Speakerphone. Then call your Bell Telephone Business Office for full particulars.

AD #5

Dry skin? Not me, darling.
Every inch of little me is as smooth as (well, you know what).
    Because I never, never bathe without Sardo.
Sardo bathes away dry skin. Gives my skin precious moisture
        (moisture is really a girl's best friend).
And Sardo works from bath to bath to keep moisture in,
        dryness out. Rough heels? Chapped knees?
    Flaky elbows? Itchy skin? Not me! I'm an
        old smoothie. (You'd never guess how old.) Next bath,
why don't you add a capful of wonderful Sardo?
    You'll be deliciously smooth all over again.
  Where do you get Sardo? At any drug
  or cosmetic counter. Where else?

AD #6

You may have tried Kraft Dinners before and been delighted at how quick and easy they are—and how unusually good. Well, wait till you taste these *new* Dinners from Kraft. They're complete, the finest of their kind, made with all the best Kraft ingredients.

Tomorrow, help yourself to the new Kraft Pizza with Cheese. Complete, from crispy crust to tomato cheese topping. Or the Spaghetti with Meat Sauce. Lots of tender juicy beef—more beef than you'd ever expect in a sauce.

Of course they're homemade good because you cook them up fresh, yourself! When *you* do that important final cooking, everything comes out fresh and full of flavor—the way you like it.

AD #7

Hollow legs love Foodarama living.

Your family will love it too!

With Foodarama's supermarket selection of foods on hand, your family enjoys better meals. You save time by shopping less . . . save money by having room for "specials." Entertaining's more fun because you can prepare everything in advance.

You never defrost Foodarama—either the refrigerator or freezer.

And Kelvinator's "No-Frost" Foodarama costs less to buy and operate than a separate refrigerator or freezer. So much better living and savings are possible because of the Kelvinator Constant Basic Improvement program. It's another way American Motors brings you more *real value* just as in Rambler cars.

AD #8

Here's the car that's all brand-new in a pleasing new size! We made Chevelle for people who like the way a small car handles and parks—yet still want wide-open spaces inside, with a good-sized trunk to match. So we put together refreshing new styling, stretch-out interior room, big choice in performance, a huge 27-cu.-ft. trunk—all in a size that's a good foot shorter than the big cars! Inside, you'll find foam-fashioned seats topped with the newest in expensive vinyls and fabrics. In most models there's a thick color-keyed carpeting that wears like iron. And a wide range of new decorator colors.

The question I am asking—is AROMA a brand of Tough Talk?—ought first to be answered impressionistically. What about the eight personalities we have just met? Are they hard men who have been around? Clearly they are not. (One, #5, is not a man at all, but a particularly silly female. More of her later.) These people simply do not present themselves as *hard*, nor do they give any hint of a violent world they could have been around in. Do they subtly *imply* an intimacy with the reader? No: their intimacy with you and me is decidedly explicit. The voices talk as if they knew us exceedingly well, and they characterize us, the reader, in specific ways. (We own a nest egg in Ad #1; we are a business executive in #4; we run the family kitchen in 6 and 7.) Do these voices tend to ignore us, as the Tough Talker does, in favor of paying attention to their own thoughts and feelings? They do not. In fact they scarcely *have* any thoughts and feelings except as these relate to *our* needs and desires. Very polite voices we have here, whose central interest is their effort to be nice to you and me.

These personalities, then, are not Tough Talkers at all, and it is clear that I am going to call them Sweet Talkers instead. Now let us inquire how their words and arrangements differ, if they do, from the words and arrangements preferred by our six Tough Talkers.

Words, their size. The Tough Talker, it will again be remembered, consistently used more monosyllables, and fewer longer words (three syllables and more), than his contemporary or elder stylists. The adwriters of AROMA are by no means so spartan. To be statistical about our tiny samplings, the frequency of monosyllables in AROMA comes to 68 per cent of the total words used; in Tough Talk it was 78 per cent and the adwriter uses longer words at about twice the frequency of the Tough Talker. This may seem a little surprising, since one hardly thinks of advertising as complex prose. Partly we can point to the adwriter's polysyllabic tradenames (Kelvinator, Speakerphone) and perhaps his taste for terms with a speciously scientific look to them. But there also seems to be some willingness on the part of AROMA voices to use words just a little elaborate, words that could not possibly appear on the first pages of *Farewell to Arms* or *All the King's Men.* There are mouth-filling adverbs like *unaccountably, meaningfully, delightfully, deliciously.* Sometimes we read a windy cliché whose faded elegance we seem invited to appreciate, like *the rarefied and mysterious world of the connoisseur* in Ad #3. You do not sell the goods, evidently, by extreme simplicity of diction. In this regard, at least, the adwriters have turned their backs on the Tough Talker.

Modifiers. An adwriter is inconceivable without modification; his product has got to be called *best-selling, delightfully different, finest, all brand-new.* It therefore follows that AROMA contains more adjectives than the low-modifying Tough Talkers habitually use. But the attentive reader will notice something peculiar about the way nouns are modified in AROMA, a particular trick of coining phrases that deserves a longer look.

One of the traditional ways in which modifiers have come into being historically is of course by transfer from other parts of speech, notably from nouns. Children who attend school become school children; trees that bear fruit become fruit trees; lamps that illuminate streets are street lamps. By this process a clumsy phrase can be shortened, perhaps strengthened. The technical name for this use of words is the "noun adjunct." Many noun adjuncts like *fruit trees* have so thoroughly entered the language that we treat them practically as single names, and some of them eventually come to be written as one word, like *landlord.*

The distinction I am making here is between a true adjective (*tall children*) and a noun adjunct (*school children*), and my method of discriminating between the two is borrowed from the practice of contemporary linguists. It is simple enough: you call a particular modifier an adjective when you can transpose the construction in which it appears into a sentence pattern using *be* or *seem*. Thus "the tall children" can be transposed into "the children are tall" or "the children seem tall." Furthermore you can inflect the modifier: *taller* children, *tallest* children. *Tall* then is a true adjective. But the noun adjunct *school children* won't work. "The children were school." "Schooler children." "The schoolest children seemed school."

There are several noun adjuncts in our samples of Tough Talk; there are many more in AROMA; there are still more, as we shall see later, in the official prose of modern organizational life. The use of this particular construction is fashionable in our time—further evidence for the point noted by scholars that the language is increasing in "nominalization" and decreasing in "predication." But why should this development be taking place? To take an example from AROMA, why do we say *decorator colors* rather than "colors preferred by decorators" or "colors invented by decorators" or "colors manufactured under the supervision of decorators"? If it's brevity we're after, the brevity has been purchased at considerable cost in clearness, for the relation between *decorator* and *colors* is woozily ambiguous.

I myself don't believe it is brevity we're after. We don't want to be brief, we only want to appear brief, we want to *seem* businesslike. Besides, there are practical advantages to ambiguity. To explain our fascination with the noun adjunct, I suggest our fascination with naming. And why do we like names? Why is it evidently more satisfactory, in our society, to name something than to say what the thing does or what it is like? Do we suffer from some mass compulsion to act as if we knew the name, in an era when our lack of absolute knowledge is a commonplace assumption? Are we compensating, in some obscure way? In any case there is no doubt that this elliptical process of name-calling has been accelerated in our time, and that many familiar noun adjuncts are associated exclusively with modern life. Here are some examples from passages we have already considered in this book: *business district, highway patrolman, Jim Crow town, dirt shoulder, world brotherhood.* Occasionally other parts of speech are similarly shifted into noun modifiers, as in *a must book,* from "Unrequired Reading" (Chapter 2).

The frequency of the noun adjunct in AROMA, however, is just about four times what it was in Tough Talk. Many of AROMA's noun adjuncts are phrases that have similarly become familiar items of modern life, like *drug counter, stock rights, decorator colors.* (I find very few of the older kinds of phrases, no street lamps, no fruit trees, no school children.) But the great difference is this: the adwriter does not confine himself to phrases with which our culture is already familiar. He himself puts into play the traditional technique of displacing nouns (or other parts of speech) in order to cook up entirely new phrases. *Foodarama living. Communications chain-of-command. Supermarket selection.* Chevrolet speaks of its *stretch-out interior room.* The Bell Company, advertising a gadget for *conference conversations* and *intercom calls,* praises the beauties of a *hands-free, group-talk, across-the-room kind of telephone.* This is all very poetical and imaginative (I'm not saying, of course, that you have to like it). Most important, though, is the fascination with naming. Consider the implication. If one says "Hungry people love the kind of living that is associated with owning a Foodarama refrigerator," one has made more or less the point that Kelvinator makes at the beginning of Ad#7. But that is not the language of the actual ad, which reads "Hollow legs love Foodarama living." Putting aside the forced whimsy of the opening phrase, the use of *Foodarama living* as a name seems to me significant. It is not an explicit metaphor, as if one were to say that a kind of living might be associated with a kind of refrigerator. Not at all: it is a named living. It exists! We have no way of knowing whether such manipulation of nouns sells refrigerators and other nice things, but somebody must think it does, because this naming device is repeated again and again throughout AROMA.

Similarly, if you speak of "the barriers that separate people because of their difficulties with language," you are referring to a familiar problem whose perplexities will continue to disturb us, probably forever. But if you coin the phrase *language barrier*, you make the problem precise and simple, by naming it, and of course by implying an analogy with "sound barrier." You can then go ahead, as Ad #2 does, and say you've broken it, and no doubt somebody will believe you.

In all of our previous passages in this book, there has been no inventiveness of just this sort. If there had been any, it would probably have looked undignified, vulgar, or cute. There are several examples of noun adjuncts, as I have noted, especially in newswriting (*business district, highway patrolman*). The only non-newswriter who uses the noun adjunct conspicuously is the author of "Unrequired Reading," our Sweet Talker of Chapter 2. This may be just coincidence, but it is certainly suggestive.

Modifiers of adjectives. Some adverbs, like *very* or *ex-*

tremely, serve the lowly purpose of beefing up the failing force of an adjective. They are called "intensifiers," and their use may be a key to attitudes about modification. It is as if the speaker were saying that a mere adjective (*good*, *fine*) were not enough to describe the beauties in question, and the phrasing has to be *very fine*, *extremely good*. AROMA has several clear-cut examples (*just right*, *much better*), and it follows that the AROMA writers are generally liberal with the modifying of modifiers—that is, with the prefixing of an adverb to the noun-modifying adjective. *Specially and delightfully different* is a nice double example, while *homemade good* displays again the adwriter's cavalier attitude toward conventional grammar. There are very few of these piled-up modifications in our other passages, though there is a nice one —*perturbingly moving*—in "Unrequired Reading." I take it that the practice of heaping adverbs onto adjectives in this manner is characteristic of AROMA and Sweet Talk, but it is decidedly not characteristic of Tough Talk.

The definite article. Most of our Tough Talkers used the determiner *the* generously; the average for all six comes to 9 per cent of all words used. I argued, in Chapter 3, that this *implied* a relation of common understanding between speaker and reader. The tough-talking speaker doesn't go out of his way for the reader; he is self-absorbed, and he merely assumes attitudes in common with his reader. The constant *the* ("you know what I mean") reinforces this assumption. The adwriter too must set up an intimate relation with his reader and force assumptions on him, but there is a difference. He *does* have to set it up, he forces the assumptions. Where the Tough Talker *implies* intimacy, the AROMA writer *states* it, works on it, and leaps right into our laps. He does not do this with a high proportion of definite articles. (Articles in the ads: 4 per cent of all words.) He does it with a battery of other weapons, which we may now consider.

Tone. In adwriting, tone is everything. The writer's problem is to fabricate an assumed reader who has to be an attractive person with whom the real reader may be expected to identify cheerfully. Second, he must be an admirer or user, or highly prospective admirer or user, of the writer's product. The assumed reader is specifically defined, with considerable detail. "Of course they're homemade good because you cook them up fresh, yourself! When *you* do that important final cooking, everything comes out fresh and full of flavor—the way you like it." (Ad #6.) That, of course, is a crude example, in which the rejoinder "I do? Are you sure? What if I hate cooking?" is unthinkable.

The frequency of the word *you* in AROMA is over twice what it was in Tough Talk. We are directly assaulted. Not only are we addressed personally by the pronoun, but we are frequently commanded in imperative verbs, or forced to respond to rhetorical questions ("Why not try . . .?"). Meanwhile every linguistic device known to man is brought to bear on the language to secure intimacy with the reader. For example we have a whole punctuation system appropriate to informal, colloquial expression. There are dashes, parentheses, exclamation marks. The physical layout of an ad, with its spacing and colors, functions also as a kind of punctuation, and of course in the whole appearance and pictorial matter of an ad there are enormous unconventional resources for informality simply not available to conventional writers.[1] The sentence structure in AROMA is exceedingly flexible and free-swinging; there are 20 instances of "sentences" that have either no subject or no main verb, what the schoolmarm calls a sentence fragment. (*Dry skin? Not me, darling.* #5.) There are only 3 such fragments in Tough Talk. The length of sentences has been reduced almost to the disappearing point. (Average length of AROMA sentences: 11 words. Average of Ad #5: less than 6 words.) Finally, the oral-speech-intimate-tone is supported by contractions (*you'll, you've*), and of these there are considerably more in AROMA than in Tough Talk.

If we ask where among the passages we have read we might find an intimate tone created by some of these devices, we could turn to the trio of recent narrators in Chapter 5, noting in particular Jack Burden's repetitions of second-person pronouns and his contractions. But the extreme spareness of Jack's vocabulary sets him far apart from AROMA's style. As I have been suggesting, among all the passages we have looked at, it seems to be the introduction to "Unrequired Reading" (Chapter 2) that can most plausibly be compared to AROMA. Consider the following figures:

	Tough Talk	Aroma	Unrequired Reading
Proportion of mono-syllables	78%	68%	66%
Proportion of longer words	5%	12%	14%
Definite articles, per 100 words	9	4.5	5.5
Noun adjuncts, per 100 words	.9	4	2
-ly adverbial modifiers, per 100 words	.4	.8	1.0
You per 100 words	1.7	4.2	3.5

There are plenty of other measurable qualities in "Unrequired Reading" and AROMA that will not bear such comparison, to be sure. And of course the samples are ridiculously tiny: a statistician would be horrified. Still, we have at least the hint that the kinds of voices we were exposed to in AROMA may have been constructed with at least some of the tools that went into the creation of our Sweet Talker of Chapter 2.

Consider again the question of tone. The Tough Talker, we have said, assumes his intimacy with the reader so blandly that he scarcely bothers about the reader at all. It is merely understood between speaker and reader that they look at the world in the same way. A review of the Tough Talkers will remind us of this implied, unstated intimacy. Even Jack Burden, with his repetitions of *you* tearing down Highway 58 in *All the King's Men,* is not referring to the reader quite directly, but simply using the pronoun in that familiar tough way as a vulgarized *one.* "To get there you follow Highway 58. . . ." The use of *you* in Sweet Talk is quite different. Recall "Unrequired Reading": "The title of this essay may strike you as a typographical error. You may be saying to yourself . . . ." As we looked at that passage in Chapter 2, we found the assumed reader to be defined fairly closely and explicitly— younger than the speaker, college-trained but not a professional academic. "I beg of you," says the sweet-professor speaker, "to forget such obligations and responsibilities." Can you catch a whiff of AROMA in that appeal? "If you're letting investment cares compete with the quiet hours—don't." You may feel a similarity there or you may not, and if you don't, no amount of playing with statistics can convince you—nor should it. But there might be something to it.

In any event the Sweet Talker may now be defined more closely. A Sweet Talker is not at all a hard man who has been around. He addresses me directly ("you"), and when he says "you" he doesn't mean just anybody, he means *me.* He is not a passionate or self-centered man, more concerned with his own feelings than with my needs and desires. On the contrary, he goes out of his way to be nice to me. He defines me as a very particular person with identifiable qualities. (This of course is a problem, for they may not be qualities I possess or desire.) He may use the rhetorical devices of informal speech (contractions, fragments, eccentric punctuation) to secure his intimacy with me. His sentence structure is simple but his vocabulary is not, or at least it lacks the Tough Talker's spareness. In other respects that have interested me here, his rhetoric shows several qualities exactly different from the Tough Talker's. He modifies generously. He has no great love for the definite article.

On the other hand, he loves to name things. If he is an adwriter he loves to make up new names for things and call things by those names. Foodarama living, that's the life. Precisely because we have been forced into positions of such intimacy, we are impelled to accept the names. And to accept the names is to buy the product, to get rid of that old refrigerator, the one that failed to provide Foodarama living.

But having said that, I add an unconventional opinion. The adwriter's rhetoric may not be so dangerous as it is often alleged to be. The know-it-all intimacy of AROMA offends me, at least, less violently than fictitious omniscience in newswriting (Chapter 4). For one thing, of course, we recognize it's an ad; our guard is up. For another, the best ads are done with such dash and good humor that some of them have built into them their own self-irony. The tone is pushed to such extreme chumminess (Not me, darling!) that it becomes parody. (Of course we may still buy the product for all that.) Many ads are composed in language that surely suggests, at least to most readers, that the words were composed in a spirit of frolicsome exaggeration.

An example of such a frolic is Ad # 1, one of the famous series of nest-egg ads. (An enormous egg, elegantly chained, is pictured in the possession of a man of means, who is engaged in some expensive leisure-time pleasure often involving boats.) "For a better way to take care of your nest egg [the ad begins], talk to the people at Chase Manhattan. So many otherwise well-ordered people unaccountably lose their touch when the subject is personal investments." The whole ad depends for its startling effect upon a time-honored and witty literary technique, that of bringing a dead metaphor (nest egg) to life. And the pictured egg is wonderfully outsize, polished, clad in its golden chain. The prose of the ad is similarly elegant and similarly exaggerated. The rather fancy adverb *unaccountably* helps set the tone. There will be no prying here into the reasons why people are so sloppy with their investments, and if you are that way too, rest assured that you are "otherwise well-ordered." "Such nuisance details as stock rights and record keeping, call dates and coupons are Chase Manhattan's dish of tea."

The assumed reader of such prose is an almost incredible character—or so it seems to me. The bland gayety with which speaker and reader dismiss stock rights and record keeping as "nuisance details" is magnificently aristocratic. *La dolce vita.* Let 'em eat cake. For all the gestures of warm intimacy, the tone is contrived and stylized. Somebody is kidding somebody, more or less in the spirit of the flashy nest-egg photograph that heads the ad. There are, no doubt, thousands of real-life people who think of stock coupons as nuisance details, but the ad's bravado in accepting such privileged sloth as perfectly normal is almost delightful. The assumptions are so extreme that the ad contains its own parody. I see this assumed author as a complex wit capable of laughing at his own language as he utters it. In fact, to use the terms of Chapter 5, he could fairly be called "unreliable."

An ad aimed at an entirely different buying audience, but

with a narrator more spectacularly unreliable, is the charming #5. Here a pert young lady is pictured in her bath, holding to her ear one of those old-fashioned new-fashionable telephone handsets. Her left hand postures affectedly somewhere in the vicinity of her just-invisible bosom. Her hair is gaily blond and sports a pink ribbon; her amused eyes, looking right offstage at you and me, are thoroughly made up; her lipstick is delicious. In sum, this kitten is just a little absurd, and perhaps the artificial frivolity of her style suggests that she knows it. Or that somebody knows it. Of course what she is saying over the phone, to an acquaintance unidentified, is far more absurd.

Dry skin ?Not me, darling.
Every inch of little me is as smooth as (well, you know what).
Because I never, never bathe without Sardo.
Sardo bathes away dry skin. Gives my skin precious moisture
(moisture is really a girl's best friend).

Here is a case, surely, where at least some readers, if not most readers, are expected to laugh at the young lady while maintaining a sympathetic touch with an assumed author who is also laughing at his creation. At the same time the assumed author is frankly selling a product! It is all quite complicated. The lady's dated clichés and general silliness are intolerable except as parody, though, doubtless, many readers of the *Ladies Home Journal* (where it appeared) read the ad, took the language straight, and bought the stuff. But the adwriter has ingeniously produced such an exaggerated tone that readers of a more critical turn of mind (you and I, dear assumed reader?) may also enjoy the ad. *And buy the stuff!* The assumed author is a very slippery fellow, with something for everybody. Even the young lady in the ad seems to have some sense of AROMA's tired phrases, and she kids them as she utters them. "Where do you get Sardo? At any drug or cosmetic counter. Where else?" We can scarcely imagine anyone, outside of an ad, actually saying "any drug or cosmetic counter." That is ad-language. But her flip question, "Where else?" undercuts it, and forces us to reconsider this young lady. Who *is* she? Is she terribly bright or terribly dumb? Who is her assumed author, how much of this is *he* making fun of? The intricacies of unreliability here are worthy of a novelist.

Questions about the narrating voice in an ad are even more pressing on television. There a voice literally speaks, and our response is governed not only by its rhetoric but by audible tone, visible facial expression, gesture, and most of the other forces of face-to-face communication mentioned in Chapter 1. Even in an ad in which the speaker does not appear on the screen, his manner of speech conveys personality and attitude—sometimes an attitude that expresses irony about his own "message."

Take the recent series of Rheingold Beer commercials, well known in New York, whose final line—we must be doing something right—has become a national cliché. A characteristic ad in this series gives us some quick shots of a Greek-American wedding, full of mirth and old-world jollity. Gay dancers of various ages are seen cooling off with bottles of New York's favorite beer. "In New York City," the voice intones (I quote from memory), "where there are more Greeks than in Sparta, more people drink Rheingold than any other brand. How come so many Greeks prefer Rheingold? We don't know, but we must be doing something right."

The illogic here must be at least subconsciously apparent to any listener; it becomes obvious if we reduce it to a syllogism.

Lots of Greeks live in New York.
Lots of New Yorkers prefer Rheingold.
Lots of Greeks prefer Rheingold.

The loophole in this line of argument is big enough to drive a beer truck through. Known to the logician as the Fallacy of the Undistributed Middle, it is a familiar type of chicanery, but rarely is it so ostentatious. I suspect that is just the point. The voice that utters all this does so with such dry urbanity that we can hardly believe he expects us to be taken in, at least by his logic. "You and I are men of this world," he *may* be saying, "and we recognize that the reasoning in this commercial is absurd. What else would we expect? But how good-humored we are about it all, how charming the Greeks are at their convivial high jinks, how charming *I* am to entertain you not only with that Greek folderol but with the very absurdity of my argument! On the whole, considering the easy gayety of this little show I've put on for you, you may as well drink Rheingold too. I mean, it can't be *that* bad!" He may be saying all that, to some of his listeners. On the other hand he may not.

The language of modern fiction and the language of modern advertising, while obviously different, and certainly paid at different rates, share at least this in common: both are produced with more care and energy and talent than any other prose in our time. If there are fresh and imaginative uses of language to be discovered, they should be here—and they are, in their different ways. And in both genres one finds *some* uses of words so self-conscious and contrived that the reader can be unsure where he is, unsure, that is, of the speaker's voice and its relation to the assumed author. Is it possible that both these arts, the novelist's and the adwriter's, are entering a rococo phase? Who's talking? Not me, darling.[2]

7

STUFFY TALK
The Rhetoric of Hollow Men

Leaning together,
Headpiece filled with straw. Alas!

The voice we hear in an ad is not the official voice of the corporation that pays the bill. The voice in the ad is a highly fictitious created person, speaking as an individual in a particular situation. In a bathtub, for instance. No corporation could ever say, officially, "I never, never bathe without Sardo." The official voice of a corporation appears, I suppose, in its periodic reports to its stockholders, or in its communications with government agencies.

I define official prose, accordingly, as language whose voice speaks for an organization rather than for an individual. And nobody says a good word for it, not even its authors. The composing of officialese suffers from circumstances, however, that make the job especially difficult, and possibly some small sympathy is in order. For just as such prose speaks for a group of people rather than for a single writer, so in its actual composition a number of people are likely to be lending a hand. And in writing, two hands are usually worse than one.[1]

Anyone who has worked on a committee preparing a document to be signed by all fellowwriters knows some of the difficulties. Disagreements of opinion and emphasis can produce a voice that is hardly a voice at all. Constant qualification makes for weakness. The various writers, all too aware of their audience as real people, may try to anticipate hopelessly conflicting prejudices and objections. Everybody has a point he wants included, but what is worse, no one feels any personal responsibility for the tone of the whole. Nobody cares, really. Contrast the situation of the single writer alone at his desk, who can establish a single speaking voice and an ideal assumed reader to listen to it. Yet a great deal of modern prose is written, or at any rate rewritten, not at a lonely desk but around a table where everybody talks at once. The loss of personality almost inevitable under such circumstances should cause us anguish whenever, as so often happens, we have to read or write the prose of organization life. When we speak of official prose as *stuffy*, we are referring, I think, directly to this loss of personality. (Not that you need a committee to produce stuffiness, and in our next chapter we shall consider some noncorporate examples.) Stuffiness may imply, by way of the stuffed shirt, that the speaker has no insides, no humanity. It is scarecrow prose. Other familiar metaphors also seem to recognize an emptiness within; thus we speak of the "inflated" language of officialese, the speaker in that case being filled with gas, or hot air.

What is the rhetoric of such hollow men, and how can it be improved, if it can?

Take a handy example, the federal government's much-publicized report, "Smoking and Health," issued early in 1964. The text quoted in the newspapers ("Summary and Conclusions") begins this way:

In previous studies the use of tobacco, especially cigarette smoking, has been causally linked to several diseases. Such use has been associated with increased deaths from lung cancer and other diseases, notably coronary artery disease, chronic bronchitis, and emphysema. These widely reported findings, which have been the cause of much public concern over the past decade, have been accepted in many countries by official health agencies, medical associations, and voluntary health organizations.

The potential hazard is great because these diseases are major causes of death and disability. In 1962, over 500,000 people in the United States died of arteriosclerotic heart disease (principally coronary artery disease), 41,000 died of lung cancer, and 15,000 died of bronchitis and emphysema.

Another cause of concern is that deaths from some of these diseases have been increasing with great rapidity over the past few decades.

Lung cancer deaths, less than 3,000 in 1930, increased to 18,000 in 1950. In the short period since 1955, deaths from lung cancer rose from less than 27,000 to the 1962 total of 41,000. This extraordinary rise has not been recorded for cancer of any other site. While part of the rising trend for lung cancers is attributable to improvements in diagnosis and the changing age-composition and size of the population, the evidence leaves little doubt that a true increase in the lung cancer has taken place.

This is by no means an extreme example of stuffiness, and I quote it to give the official voice its due. And I reaffirm my modest sympathy with the authors, who must have had to compose this document under difficult circumstances. There were ten of them on the committee, professional experts chosen by the Surgeon General, presumably strong-minded men of varying opinions. A separate committee staff was also involved. There must have been considerable debate about phrasing as well as more "substantial" matters, and no doubt uneasy compromises had to be made. A consciousness of audience must have been high in the writers' minds. On one hand the document had to be acceptable to the scientific community, particularly to those scientists who had participated in various earlier projects on which this report was based. On another hand, the document was surely addressed to legislators and officials with the expectation of their taking the "remedial action" called for. On still a third hand, these multidextrous writers must have wished to reach the smoking public directly, and they surely anticipated the reprinting of key passages like this one in the daily press. We may, as I say, sympathize with the practical difficulties of multiple authorship and multiple readership, but it does not follow that we have to like the results. For this is a Stuffy voice.

For a harder look at the created personality, I take a shorter passage from a page in the committee's report where one might suppose both writer and reader to be especially attentive. It is a point where, if anywhere, the committee might be expected to speak directly and plainly, with a minimum of hot air.[2] Here is the much-quoted conclusion under the heading "Lung Cancer":

Cigarette smoking is causally related to lung cancer in men; the magnitude of the effect of cigarette smoking far outweighs all other factors. The data for women, though less extensive, point in the same direction.

The risk of developing lung cancer increases with duration of smoking and the number of cigarettes smoked per day, and is diminished by discontinuing smoking.

The risk of developing cancer of the lung for the combined group of pipe smokers, cigar smokers, and pipe and cigar smokers is greater than for nonsmokers, but much less than for cigarette smokers.

The data are insufficient to warrant a conclusion for each group individually.

"Cigarette smoking is causally related to lung cancer in men. . . ." Causally related? Probably there is some good reason why the committee could not say simply "Cigarette smoking causes lung cancer in men." What good reason could there be? Perhaps the latter phrasing suggests that smoking is the *only* cause of lung cancer? Perhaps it suggests that all smoking necessarily causes lung cancer? But our faint understanding of the committee's anxiety for caution and clarity, in the light of its complex audience, should not prevent us from deploring the alternative. For by using the passive verb (*is related to*) and its odd modifier (*causally*), the writers deprive their language not only of strength but of responsibility. Note that in this sentence the committee's voice isn't doing any relating itself; all it's saying is that something is or has been related to something—by someone else. Very scientific, very "objective." Then we read on (to finish the first sentence): "the magnitude of the effect far outweighs all other factors." The magnitude is doing the outweighing, not the austere members of this committee. The choice of language in the following sentence ("data . . . point in the same direction") is of course similar. An abstraction (data) is pointing, not a human finger. Explained in these terms, we can understand why the voice in this first paragraph sounds so disembodied and the wording sounds so awkward.[3]

A key characteristic of Stuffy rhetoric is just this refusal to assume personal responsibility. It is accomplished by at least two stylistic techniques, both of which we have just witnessed. One is the use of the passive verb. (Military prose, among others, is full of this gambit: *it is ordered that . . . it is desired that.* . . . Who ordered, who desired? With such rhetoric, buck-passing becomes child's play.) The other technique is a preference for abstract nouns as the subjects of active verbs. The doer of the action is not a human somebody, certainly not the speaker himself. It is Magnitude, or Data, buzzing along while the speaker merely notes the unarguable results.

It is as if the speaker, in this first paragraph, had made a determined effort to keep *people* out of the discussion, including himself. Whether this was done to promote a kind of official tone for the sake of legislators, or to sound mathematical and cautious for the sake of scientists, or simply out of stuffy habit, I cannot tell. But the effort partly breaks down in the second paragraph. "The risk of developing lung cancer increases with duration of smoking." This is still clothed in pretty abstract dress, but there has been a significant change, for now we are suddenly seeing the situation almost from an individual smoker's point of view. The statement seems far less rigorously mathematical when the subject of the sentence is a word like *risk*, though of course the riskiness is based on numbers. And the writers' own risk seems abruptly much greater, for now they do seem to be taking responsibility for a more ambitious assertion: "the risk increases." It is hard to understand why they had to be so awkwardly impersonal and cautious in their first paragraph, if they were going to come out so flatly in their second.

In the third paragraph the voice continues, rather woodenly, with "risk," and then moves into a terrible tangle as the writers, trying to deal with three groups of smokers, produce an almost unreadable mess. "Pipe smokers, cigar smokers, and pipe and cigar smokers." This sort of thing is easily perpetrated by a voice that cares as little about its reader as this one does. Then in the final sentence of the passage the voice backs away again into its posture of impersonal no-responsibility. "The data are insufficient to warrant a conclusion. . . ." Data are insufficient only if somebody says so. Once again, the subject of the verb is the data, not the interpreters of the data.

No doubt the data are insufficient to warrant a conclusion, but I find insurmountable the temptation to rewrite the committee's prose into plainer English, and politer.

Cigarette smoking is the major cause of lung cancer in men, and probably in women too.

The longer one smokes, and the more cigarettes one smokes per day, the greater the chance of developing lung cancer. This risk is reduced when one stops smoking.

People who smoke pipes or cigars, or both, also risk cancer, but to a lesser degree than cigarette smokers. We cannot say exactly what the risk is for each of these groups.

For any number of reasons, possibly even good reasons, this version might be unacceptable to the advisory committee. But at least we can examine some of the ways in which the revision was accomplished, and so focus on some rhetorical characteristics of Stuffiness. In the first place, of course, human responsibility has been introduced, in the opening sentence, by the simple tactic of removing the passive verb and making a more positive statement. (The statement *seems* to be justified by the original.) The original's willingness to speak of "the risk" in its second paragraph is retained in the revision, and the smoker's own involvement in the situation is further encouraged by the introduction of "people" in the revised third paragraph. Finally, the committee's responsibility is made explicit in the revised last sentence, by changing "The data are insufficient to warrant. . ." into "We cannot say exactly what. . . ."

These changes suggest that I have tried to make a scarecrow into a human being. By what other means can one humanize the quality of a Stuffy voice? One way is to reduce sharply the sheer number of words, in this case by something over one-quarter. Stuffy voices talk too much, although for sheer gratuitous verbosity a Sweet voice does pretty well too. The Stuffy voice characteristically uses longer words, and the revision shows a clear rise in proportion of monosyllables, and an even clearer drop in proportion of words of more than two syllables. Stuffy voices modify nouns almost as generously as adwriters, and they are exceedingly fond of the noun adjunct construction. Whereas the original contained nine adjectives and nine noun adjuncts (like *cigarette smoking*), the revision contains three of each. Finally, repetition in the original is very high (the "wooden" effect alluded to), and this repetition, while still present in the revision, has been reduced. A list of this information may be of interest:

	Original	*Revision*
Total number of words	106	76
Average sentence length	21	15
Proportion of monosyllables	57%	69%
Proportion of words over two syllables	18%	5%
Adjectives and noun adjuncts	18	6

Such "rules" as these figures suggest are familiar enough, and many a popular treatise on writing has been based on the simpleminded proposition that simple words and sentences are always better than complex ones.[4] But that is not the point at all. It depends! In true Stuffy Talk, we feel a disparity between the simplicity of the situation, as we feel it ought to be defined, and the pretentiousness of the lingo. As so often in literary matters, we have to appeal finally to extraliterary considerations—our sense of a "proper" definition of the circumstances. Thus we resent a voice haranguing us from a high horse, not just because his horse is high, but because the situation seems to us to be worthy of a more modest perch. If you are composing a preamble to a new nation's constitution, you have a perfect right to climb up on a high horse.[5] On the other hand, if you're trying to get people to stop smoking. . . .

But this is not to say at all that the problem of cancer and smoking is frivolous: the tone of my revision remains serious, even though I have brought the voice down from on high and into closer contact with the listener. I did not go so far as to invoke the intimacy of the Sweet Talker, or even the Tough Talker. The occasion remains, at it must, official and formal. Nevertheless it is true that in revising I have imposed upon the committee's style some of the Tough Talker's manners. A little Tough Talk goes a long way, sometimes, as an antidote to Stuffy Talk, and I have no doubt that most committee reports would be more palatable if the language could be brought somewhat into line with Tough Talk's rhetoric. But easy does it. Whereas a little Toughness can be wholesome, a little Sweetness can be sickening. How facile it would be to reduce an official voice to mere cuteness, in a flurry of public-relations informality. For instance take this sentence from the original committee report:

The risk of developing lung cancer increases with duration of smoking and the number of cigarettes smoked per day, and is diminished by discontinuing smoking.

My revision offered this alternative:

The longer one smokes, and the more cigarettes one smokes per day, the greater the chance of developing lung cancer. This risk is reduced when one stops smoking.

A reviser interested in promoting informality could easily become too interested. He could, for instance, bring the voice still closer to the reader by the simple introduction of the second-person pronoun:

The longer you smoke, and the more cigarettes you smoke per day, the greater your chance of developing lung cancer. This risk is reduced when you stop smoking.

This begins now to look like the clubbiness of Sweet Talk—a degree of admonitory intimacy that the members of the committee would no doubt, and rightly, consider beneath their dignity. And from here it is only a step to the full saccharine flavor of Sweet Talk itself:

No doubt about it—when you smoke cigarettes you're running a scientifically-proved risk of lung cancer. That is, if you're a man. And if you're a woman, you're probably running a risk that's almost as certain.

Fact is, the longer you've smoked, and the more cigarettes you smoke every day, the likelier you are to develop cancer. But scientific data demonstrate that you can lower that risk any time you care to—just stop smoking.

If you smoke cigars or a pipe (or both), you're still risking cancer. But a good deal less than you are if you stick to those cigarettes.

So why not cut out expensive, evil-smelling, disease-laden cigarette smoking for good? Like the Surgeon General says you should.

Examples of Stuffy Talk abound. Of our three styles, it is the easiest to recognize and define; perhaps it is easy to compose too. Consider another example, from another branch of government. Not long ago the pay envelopes of academicians included a document stating a new ruling by the Internal Revenue Service. This ruling, a welcome one to its recipients, concerned certain deductible expenses on the part of professors. It began this way; and it needs no comment:

REVENUE

Advice has been requested concerning the deductibility for Federal income tax purposes of research expenses, including traveling expenses, incurred by college and university professors in their capacity as educators.

The facts presented are that the duties of a professor encompass not only the usual lecture and teaching duties but also the communication and advancement of knowledge through research and publication. Appointments are commonly made to college and university faculties with the expectation that the individuals involved will carry on independent research in their fields of competence and will put that research to use in advancing the body of learning in that area by teaching, lecturing, and writing. It is customary, therefore, for professors to engage in research for the above purposes. Where the research is undertaken with a view to scholarly publication, the expenses for such purposes cannot usually be considered to have been incurred for the purpose of producing a specific income-producing asset . . . .

Based on the facts presented, it is held that research expenses, including traveling expenses properly allottable thereto, incurred by a professor for the purposes of teaching, lecturing, or writing and publishing in this area of competence, as a means of carrying out the duties expected of him in his capacity as a professor and without expectation of profit apart from his salary, represent ordinary and necessary business expenses incurred in that capacity and are therefore deductible under section 162(e) of the Code.

I take a final example of Stuffy Talk from another end of academic life. Here is the voice of the academic institution itself, a passage from the catalogue of a liberal arts college setting forth its policy on admissions.

ADMISSIONS

Admission to X College is a selective process, since each year many more qualified candidates apply for admission than can possibly be accommodated. In considering the factors involved in the selections, academic ability, and achievement, community citizenship and leadership, character, and personality are considered most important. Special emphasis is placed on the candidate's record of achievement throughout his secondary school years. Specifically, selection of candidates is based on information obtained from the following sources: (1) the secondary school record, including rank in class; (2) the College Entrance Examination Board's Scholastic Aptitude and Achievement Tests; (3) a personal interview with a member of the Admissions staff, or with a designated representative; (4) the recommendation of the school.

X College admits undergraduates for the Bachelor of Arts degree only. For practical reasons of adjustment to college life and the proper arrangements of a program of study, X admits freshman students only in September, at the beginning of the fall semester. The freshman class is limited by the capacity of the dormitories. An early application is advised. It is expected that candidates who live within a reasonable distance of the College will visit X sometime before January of their senior year of secondary school.

The Admissions office is open for appointments throughout the year except on Saturday afternoons and Sundays. (During the months of July and August appointments and interviews are not scheduled on Saturdays.) An appointment with the Admissions Officer may be arranged by writing or phoning the Admissions Office at least two weeks in advance of the intended visit.

As every parent, teacher, and teenager knows, admission to college these days is a desperate business. But the assumed author here could hardly care less. Certainly he admits no difficulties on his part, and his passive verbs do their efficient work of evading responsibility. "Special emphasis *is placed*. . ., selection of candidates *is based* . . ." Note that it is quite possible to be Stuffy within a very short sentence: "An early application *is advised*." In the face of all these passives, the poor applicant has nobody to argue with. The machine grinds on. There is no hint here about what actually happens in the "admissions process"—who pores over the documents, how he or they do make decisions, what the relative importance may be of the four sources of information. Furthermore an interview with an Officer whose very title rates a capital O is already a formidable undertaking. Surely teenagers have enough troubles, without having to face the blank face of prose like this.

8

BEING SERIOUS WITHOUT BEING STUFFY
Some Practical Advice

It struck him abruptly that a woman whose only being
was to "make believe" . . . was a kind of monster.
                                            —*The Tragic Muse*

The three styles I have been trying to describe inevitably give
rise to questions of value. Which is it best to be—a Tough or
a Sweet or a Stuffy Talker? While many would perhaps not
object to being labeled Tough—possibly remembering William James' honorific use of the word—few would want to be
called either Sweet or Stuffy. Actually, all three extremes are
dangerous. Though it is clearly possible to write very well
within the limits of the Tough style, it is easy to write badly
too, to sound not simply curt but moronic. Every cheap who-
dunit will testify to the indulgence in mindlessness and ego
that the Tough style makes easy. As for Sweet Talk and Stuffy
Talk, it is difficult to imagine first-rate writing composed
strictly within those manners, except as parody. At least I
have found no extreme Sweet or Stuffy passage that I can
also admire as literature, unless we count such *jeux d'esprit* as

the Sardo girl of Ad # 5. The Style Sampler of my appendix will show the variety of bad writing that is possible under Sweet and Stuffy rubrics.

I submit, then, that all three of our styles are dangers in modern prose, in ascending order of peril. As a Tough Talker, it is all too easy to sound egocentric, or simpleminded, or plain vulgar. As a Sweet Talker, it is hard to avoid sounding chummy in a way to make most discriminating readers recoil. And as a Stuffy Talker it is almost impossible *not* to sound as if you didn't care about your reader at all.

These difficulties are pervasive in modern American writing, perhaps in any writing. They are apparent, for example, in the styles of those who pontificate on style itself. Let us try a few more passages, this time from the discourse of language experts talking about language.

In the last few years there have appeared on the textbook market a number of anthologies of essays about language and usage. These have been extraordinarily similar in purpose, they have been aimed at an identical audience, and they share current fashionable attitudes of the modern linguistic scholar. They provide us, therefore, with something of a laboratory situation for measuring difference in style. What kinds of voice can we identify in the styles of the anthologists themselves? How do they share the difficulties of self-expression that we have been observing in novelists, journalists, adwriters, and committee spokesmen? All we need, for a tentative answer, is a look at the first hundred words or so of their prefaces.

Here is one:

From the early grades through the first year of college, the textbooks in grammar and usage scarcely change. The repetition is well meant and apparently necessary: if they won't learn what's good for them, make them do it again. Certainly habits are

formed and re-formed by repetitive drill, but it is clear from the
record that repetition is not enough.

This book is based on the conviction that knowledge must be
added to drill so that repetition may open into growth. Everyone
aims at this, at confidence and pleasure in the use of language
rather than at anxiety about being correct; the problem has been
to get the liberating knowledge, which is scattered through books
and journals, into the hands of the students.

A reader who thinks first about details of grammar, and only
second of his impression of the whole voice, may too quickly
assume that we have a Stuffy Talker here. The reader, that
is to say, who has read the last chapter *too* thoroughly, might
tick off those verbs in the passive voice and say, There it is—
Stuffy. For there they are: *is well meant, are formed and re-
formed, is based, must be added, is scattered.* Nevertheless, as
any sensible reader will point out, this is *not* a Stuffy voice
at all—quite the contrary. Perhaps it is almost too breezy. In
any case the barrage of passive verbs here is simply not
enough to overcome all the other stylistic tricks in this passage
which propel the tone in quite another direction, toward
Toughness and Sweetness.

What are they? For one thing, the wry half-quotation, *if
they won't learn what's good for them. . . ,* with its colloquial
flavor, serves to disarm the reader in the very second sentence. The willingness to include such talk, in a kind of jocular
spirit, is part of a general modesty on the part of the speaker,
who is at pains to remind us that there is something to be
said for the opposition. "The repetition is well meant," he ac-
knowledges. "Everyone aims at this, at confidence and pleasure in the use of language"—not just I in my wisdom. In
sum, the voice here is not that of a Stuffy lecturer at all, but
represents some mixture of my three styles.

A short time after the anthology prefaced in this manner

appeared, another similar collection was published whose preface begans as follows:

The basic premise of this collection of essays is that language in and of itself is an important subject for study. The second, and equally important, premise is that one can learn about language by reading a variety of essays oriented to the best that modern scholars have thought and said about it.

Because the study of English is often atomized, it is effectively divorced from the broad and scholarly concerns that it is uniquely able to illuminate. In his study of language under the guise of composition, grammar, rhetoric, or poetics, the student is seldom made to think about the nature of language itself.

I hope my reader may sense the difference in that voice, before he stops to take note of details that may account for the difference. The voice here, as I hope we may agree, is less brisk, more removed from the reader, with an academic manner of address that suggests some lack of excitement about what it's saying. If that judgment is at all fair, we may then ask, where does this manner come from? Why is this man so different, even though in realistic fact he is attempting to talk to the same audience for an almost identical purpose?

There are plenty of concrete differences; some of them may be persuasive. The vocabulary of our second speaker is more pretentious, with more longer words and far fewer monosyllables. There are fewer independent verbs, resulting in more subordination, both clauses and other dependent structures. (Half the passage occurs inside subordinate clauses.) There is a tendency to interrupt normal sentence patterns, to make the reader wait for further modification. "The basic premise *of this collection of essays* is. . . ." The second, *and equally important*, premise is. . . ." The tag about the best thought and said may be deliberately ironic, but it's a tired tag for all that. These and other habits of speech may partially justify our feeling that the second anthologist is more dryly professorial (if not plain duller) than the first.

Now here is a third, introducing still another collection of similar essays, aimed at the same audience. It may be his sense of the competition that makes this writer speak as he does.

> The growth of interest in language study, in linguistics, has been one of the interesting intellectual developments of the twentieth century. Linguistics must now be viewed as an established and independent branch of study. Under the circumstances it would be odd if there were not a number of books issued to introduce this study to the general public and to the university undergraduate. Many excellent collections of language articles and selections for the undergraduate—especially for the freshman —have appeared in recent years. The compiler of still another collection is consequently obliged to indicate why he adds his product to the number available.[1]

Anyone who begins a book by telling us that "the growth of interest" in something is an "interesting development" cannot himself be overwhelmingly interested in what he has to say. In any event, those rhetorical habits of Stuffiness that we associate with a remoteness from both subject and audience are here apparent. The vocabulary is now even more multisyllabic. There are fewer finite verbs, with consequent subordination of much of the language. Passive verbs are actually less frequent than in our first passage, but other significant habits appear—for instance the noun adjunct. We have *language study, university undergraduates, language articles*— clear hints that we are approaching the jargon of officialese. The interrupted sentence patterns are interesting; here the writer habitually places modifying phrases between his subject and verb, letting his reader wait patiently until he is all through qualifying. The writer's reference to himself as "the compiler of still another collection" may be taken as a symptom of his nervous self-consciousness. His reaction to his nervousness is withdrawal.

The paragraph I have quoted is followed by a sentence beginning "It is hoped that this book may be welcome for three main reasons. . . ." It is to be wondered who's doing the hoping. Could it be by any chance the author himself? Is there then some good reason why he shouldn't say so? This man seems to be running scared.

The major fault in modern prose generally is Stuffiness. It is true that Sweetness too can be very offensive; witness the overlays of Sweetness on Toughness that, in Chapter 4, I argued were observable in the contemporary novel. The excess of Sweetness in journalism (see the Style Sampler) speaks for itself. For most people, though, in most situations, in the writing of everyday serious expository prose, it is the Stuffy voice that gets in the way. The reason it gets in the way, I submit, is that the writer is scared: If this is an age of anxiety, one way we react to our anxiety is to withdraw into omniscient and multisyllabic detachment where nobody can get us.

No book, certainly not this book, can remove a person's anxiety for him. But it may be that, through a study of style, one might remove some *symptoms* of anxiety from one's prose. Therefore it may not be utterly useless to offer a little Practical Advice, most of it fairly obvious, for avoiding the symptoms of Stuffiness. To follow such advice may amount to little more than taking aspirin: it may reduce the headache without touching the anxiety. And yet, if anxiety is found in the style of our language, perhaps changing our style may be the best thing we can do. In any case, here are some Rules, deduced from this study, for avoiding the Stuffy voice, at least as that voice is defined in this book.

HOW TO AVOID BEING STUFFY

1. Make about two-thirds of your total vocabulary mono-syllabic; keep words of three syllables or more down to under 20 per cent.

2. Try making some of the subjects of your verbs *people*, not neuter nouns.

3. Manage a *finite verb* about every ten words, on the average. (Which is more than that sentence does.)

4. Don't overuse the *passive voice*. (But don't avoid it altogether either.)

5. Keep down the *noun adjuncts*.

6. Keep the average length of *subordinate clauses* down to ten words or so, and see to it that the total proportion of subordinate clauses runs to no more than a third of the whole.

7. Most marks of *punctuation* (except commas and semi-colons) serve to lighten tone. Consider question marks, parentheses, italics, dashes, and of course exclamations.

8. Don't *interrupt* subject and verb with intervening sub-ordinate constructions and modifiers.

9. If really desperate, try a *contraction* or two, or a *fragment* (verbless sentence).

10. Whatever you do, *don't obey all these rules at once*, for to do so would be to emerge with something disastrously cute, probably on the Sweet side. The careful writer, in fact, carefully *dis*obeys some of these rules, precisely to avoid the pose of sickly Sweetness. He includes a passive verb, now and then, a lengthy subordinate clause, an elegant interruption between subject and verb. Perhaps his

skill in making such choices is what we mean by a *balanced style.*

It remains to say a word about the moral side of rhetoric. The three styles I have been trying to describe can be called ways of making believe. Any style, any way of thinking, can be regarded as a make-believe performance, and it is always possible to take comfort by distinguishing between the performance on the one hand and the Real Person that stands behind all the play-acting on the other. That's not me, that's just my voice of the moment. But such a distinction breaks down very soon; even in the writing of fiction, as we have seen, it produces difficulties. And in the course of our day-to-day lives, we have to live with the effects of our performances. The voices I choose are mine, my responsibility, and the belief I own up to is the make-believe I have made. Serious play-acting. The world is not a stage, nor ever was.

Put that way, all three styles I have been examining are, as I have said, dangerous. Exceedingly common as they are in modern American life, they suggest three ways in which Americans upstage one another. One can talk Tough, beating the hairy chest, and make a spectacle of one's ostentatious simplicity. See how true and humble I am, more true and humble than you are. (And sometimes, furthermore, I really Know!) Or one can talk Sweet, leaping into the lap of one's listener, however unwanted there. See how nice I am to you, you boob. Or one can talk Stuffy, laying down the law as if one were Moses and all the world were a wandering tribe looking for the Word. In each case the rhetoric, all too often, creates a character who is ill-mannered, to say no worse of him. He has lost forbearance and restraint, a regard for the feelings of his listeners. The result is that in our time we are fairly surrounded by voices that are not much fun to be with.

At the beginning of our first chapter, we noted how our
sense of a person, in an ordinary social introduction, is not
simply a matter of words, but a matter of many different
physical impressions. Gesture and grimace, voicebox and eyelid are all rich with meaning. In written prose, though, it is all
words, and the business of the modern day is performed, much
of it, with written words. For some people, actions in written
language are the principal actions of their lives—at least of
their professional lives. Handsome is as handsome writes. But
how few of us write handsomely! Instead, the characters we
create for ourselves, the characters we become, are too often
egocentric and ill-mannered. We push one another around.
(Examples abound, I know, in the style of this book, this
chapter, this sentence.) And the ill manners can be produced
by, among other things, an excessive Toughness, or Sweetness,
or Stuffiness, particularly the latter two.

The excesses are understandable. In the very act of addressing someone we acknowledge a wish to push him around, and
in our zeal to push a little harder, it is no wonder our voices
begin to sound strident. It is with style that we try to behave
like a decent person, one who ruefully concedes his drive for
power while remaining aware of his reader's well-chosen re-
sistance. Thus style is our way of becoming a person worth
listening to, worth knowing.

A moral justification for the study of rhetoric lies right here.
We improve ourselves by improving the words we write. We
make our performance less monstrous, by *acting* like human
beings. Just what comprises a satisfactory human performance
is every man's complicated decision. But at least, by looking
at rhetoric, we may begin to know more about who it is we
are making believe we are. And then, perhaps, we can do
something about it.

APPENDIXES

NOTES

INDEX

APPENDIX A

STYLES AND STATISTICS
A Model T Style Machine

A recognition of the dual and complementary value of
intuitive judgment of language use on the one hand,
and the more objective techniques of description of
language phenomena which modern linguistics makes
available on the other, is necessary and indeed fundamental to this view of stylistic study.
—John Spencer and Michael Gregory,
Linguistics and Style (London, 1964)

Out of the various observations we have made about our three
styles, is it possible—is it even proper—to construct a system-
atic grammar and rhetoric for each? No, possibly not. Nevertheless what follows is an effort to make a beginning in that
direction. I offer here a kind of Style Machine, of a pre-Model
T order, designed to measure the tone of a prose passage. It
considers only a tiny fraction of the possibilities, it will not
discriminate between good and bad writing, it is full of bugs.
Much of its terminology is hopelessly square, derived from
traditional grammar at least as much as from modern linguistics. But it will serve at least to summarize some of the
distinctions setting Tough Talk apart from Sweet Talk and

from Stuffy Talk, and it may furthermore suggest to somebody else a way of improving on this primitive beginning.

Let us first see where we have been. We have at hand about three thousand words of prose, approximately equally divided among the three styles. (We have also read several passages—Eliot, Howells, the *Times* and *Tribune,* Dickens—that we did not classify in any such category). For Tough Talk, we have, once again, the following six items:

"Private World"—an introduction to a *Saturday Review* article on the teaching of reading. (Chapter 2)

"Frederic Henry"—the opening of A *Farewell to Arms.* (Chapter 3)

"Time"—the opening of a report on Birmingham from *Time.* (Chapter 4)

"Augie March"—the opening of *The Adventures of Augie March.* (Chapter 5)

"Jack Burden"—the opening of *All the King's Men.* (Chapter 5)

"Earl Horter"—the opening of *Love Among the Cannibals.* (Chapter 5)

For Sweet Talk, we have nine items:

"Unrequired Reading"—introduction to another *Saturday Review* article on the teaching of reading. (Chapter 2)

About a hundred words each from eight miscellaneous advertisements in current magazines. (Chapter 6)

Our collection of Stuffy Talk includes:

"Teaching Literature"—still another passage on the teaching of reading, from an educator's textbook. (Chapter 2)

"Smoking"—two passages from the 1964 Surgeon General's report on smoking and cancer. (Chapter 7)

"Revenue"—a passage from a ruling by the Internal Revenue Service. (Chapter 7)

"Admissions"—a passage from a college catalogue. (Chapter 7)

The classification of these passages into the three categories was made, in the first place, impressionistically. That is, it was a question simply as to whether our reading experience brought us into contact with a speaker or voice of the indicated type. The types of individuals we were looking for, to repeat, were defined briefly like this: (1) a hard fellow who has been around in a violent world and who pays us very little mind; (2) an affable fellow who is explicitly familiar with us and who knows just who we are; (3) a bloodless fellow who often speaks for an organization and not for himself, and who keeps his distance from us.

How are these impressions of personalities to be explained in terms of grammar and rhetoric—if they are?

Out of dozens of possibilities, I propose sixteen grammatical-rhetorical qualities as ways of isolating styles, of accounting for distinctions that we feel in the voices addressing us. Several of them we have already considered at some length. I put them in the form of questions.

A. QUESTIONS ABOUT WORD-SIZE

1. What is the proportion of monosyllables in the passage?

2. What is the proportion of words of more than two syllables?

B. QUESTIONS ABOUT SUBSTANTIVES

3. How many first- and second-person pronouns does the passage contain? How many imperatives are there (*"you* understood")?
4. Are the subjects of the finite verbs mostly neuter nouns, or do they refer to people?

C. QUESTIONS ABOUT VERBS

5. What is the proportion of finite verbs to total words?
6. What proportion of these finite verbs are forms of *to be?*
7. What proportion of these verbs are in the passive voice?

D. MODIFIERS

8. What proportion of the total words are true adjectives?
9. How many of these adjectives are themselves modified by adverbs?
10. What proportion of the total words are noun adjuncts?

E. SUBORDINATION

11. What is the average length of the subordinate ("included") clauses?
12. What proportion of the total passage is inside such clauses?
13. How frequently are subject and main verb separated by intervening subordinate structures? How long are these interruptions?

F. OTHER EFFECTS OF TONE

14. How frequent is the determiner *the?*

15. Are there any sentences without subjects, or without verbs, or both? Are there any contractions?

16. How many occurrences are there of these marks of punctuation: parentheses, italics, dashes, question marks, exclamation points?

I now consider each of these questions in detail, with some statistics from my samples.

A. QUESTIONS ABOUT WORD-SIZE

Answers to the questions in this section involve nothing fancier than a simple counting of syllables. Does the word contain one syllable only, or is it composed of three or more? This kind of distinction is commonplace in popular and commercial handbooks of style, to determine the "difficulty" of prose passages: Very Difficult, Easy and so on. (See note 1, Chapter 8.) It is a useful statistic so far as it goes, but it does not go very far, for obviously a tone is not produced by word-size alone.

To decide what a syllable is, I have innocently trusted my own ear, while conceding that a strict count of morphemes would probably be more satisfactory. I doubt that the relative results would very different, however.

It may be wondered why, since I am comparing word-size, I do not compare sentence-size as well. Surely we might expect the Tough Talker to use short sentences, the Sweet Talker even shorter sentences, the Stuffy Talker longer ones. To a degree all that is true, but I have nevertheless discarded the length of sentences as a crucial factor. The differences between the styles are surprisingly small, actually. As we have seen— "Admissions," Chapter 7—it is evidently possible to sound Stuffy in short sentences, just as one can sound Tough in longer sentences. Jack Burden, for instance, utters the longest sentence in the whole collection.

1. *What is the proportion of monosyllables in the passage?*

As we have indicated several times, and as common sense would suggest, the Tough Talker uses a high proportion of monosyllables, the Stuffy Talker uses a low proportion of them. For our samples, the facts are 78 per cent for Tough Talk and 58 per cent for Stuffy Talk. The extremes in each direction are Jack Burden at 86 per cent and the official voice of "Admissions" at 50 per cent. The adwriter's Sweet Talk, as we discovered in Chapter 6, is *not* drastically simple, at least in this respect, the proportion of monosyllables falling exactly in between the two others, at 68 per cent. For extreme intimacy of tone, in other words, you do not choose a ruthlessly spartan diction, but a more flexible vocabulary that permits a wide range.

2. *What is the proportion of words of more than two syllables?*

Here of course we have just the opposite gradation, with Tough Talk at 5 per cent, Sweet Talk at 12 per cent, Stuffy Talk at 26 per cent. Extremes are Frederic Henry at 1 per cent and the voice of the Revenue Service at 29 per cent. These two people are only just speaking the same language!

Without exception all six of our Tough Talkers in the samples fall well under 10 per cent in their use of words of more than two syllables; all four Stuffy Talkers are over 20 per cent in this category. Most of the Sweet Talkers fall into a 10-19 per cent bracket, though a conspicuous exception is the lady in the bath of Ad #5. Her vocabulary is as rigorously simple as any Tough Talker's, though in most other respects she is surely Sweet.

B. QUESTIONS ABOUT SUBSTANTIVES

I consider here only the incidence of certain personal pronouns, and a single distinction with respect to the subjects of verbs. Obviously this is a vast area for further investigation. The abstract-concrete issue might be raised, though as we saw in Chapter 3 the distinction is not simple. The question of derivation (Anglo-Saxon vs. Latin), which I have not faced at all, might be relevant here.

The relative frequency of all substantives in my samples seems to be about the same for all three styles, though of course other samples might prove otherwise. Tough and Sweet Talk, however, are far more generous with pronouns than Stuffy Talk is. The Stuffy Talker tends to repeat his nouns, in a legalistic way, rather than relying on pronouns, as if he didn't trust his reader to make the proper reference. The Stuffy Talker purports to be unquestionably clear at all times, at the expense of variety and grace. But the whole measurement of repetition must wait for someone with more arithmetical patience than I have.

3. *How many first- and second-person pronouns does the passage contain? How many imperatives ("you understood")?*

The Tough Talker, we argued, is a character who, for all his implied intimacy with the assumed reader, often reveals himself to be more concerned with his own attitudes and feelings. The Sweet Talker, on the other hand, makes explicit gestures to the reader, calling him by name (*you*). The Stuffy Talker mentions neither himself nor his reader. Putting it too baldly, as I do in my preface, Tough Talk tends to be I-Talk, Sweet Talk tends to be You-Talk, Stuffy Talk tends to be It-

Talk. My figures don't quite justify that statement, but let it stand. Of the 30 first-person pronouns in our samples, 16 are in Tough Talk, 12 in Sweet Talk, 2 in Stuffy Talk. There are 63 instances of the word *you*: 21 in Tough Talk, 42 in Sweet Talk, none at all in Stuffy Talk. In addition there are 8 instances of imperative verbs in Sweet Talk, with the subject *you* "understood."[1]

The word *I* excludes the reader, the word *you* includes him. The word *we* can work either way: it may mean "those people and I, but not you, reader," or it may mean "everybody, including you and me," or it may mean, *à deux*, "you and I, dear reader." I take it that the last meaning ought to be characteristic of Sweet Talk, even though I find no examples in my collection. In fact the only use of the first-person-plural pronoun to include the reader at all occurs in Earl Horter.

4. *Are the subjects of the finite verbs mostly neuter nouns, or are they nouns referring to people?*

The distinctions here depend to some extent, of course, on what the speaker is talking about: it is predictable that a first-person-singular narrator in a novel should talk about people while the Internal Revenue Service should be concerned with facts and figures. But style matters too, as we can appreciate by returning once more to those first three passages of Chapter 2. There we encountered three voices, each talking more or less about the same "thing," but each using a different style. (I ignore, for a moment, the fourth passage, Mr. Eliot's.) In those three passages two-thirds of the grammatical subjects in "Teaching Literature" (Stuffy) were neuter, two-thirds of the subjects in "Unrequired Reading" (Sweet) were human beings, and "Private World" (Tough) divided its subjects exactly evenly between neuter nouns and people. It simply makes a difference how you say what you say—for example, how you state a conclusion. You can say "I believe . . .," or you can say "You will understand . . .," or you can say "The facts demonstrate. . . ." By such choices you create your voice.

The totals in all my samples are as follows: Tough Talk, 52 neuter subjects of finite verbs, 72 people; Sweet Talk, 45 neuters and 70 people; Stuffy Talk, 52 neuters and only 12 people. Two Tough Talkers and two ads (Henry, Earl Horter, Ads 7 and 8) are exceptional in using more neuter subjects than human beings. All Stuffy Talkers use at least two-thirds neuter nouns as their subjects. This concentration on the nonhuman in Stuffy Talk, as the doer of the action, contributes largely to the general air of no-personal-responsibility that I advanced in Chapter 7.

C. QUESTIONS ABOUT VERBS

Under this heading I am considering finite verbs only—no participles, no gerunds, no infinitives. All these deserve attention to see how Stuffy Talk compensates for its paucity of finite verbs. There is also work to be done, as indicated below, with auxiliaries and base verbs.

5. *What is the proportion of finitive verbs to total words?*

The distinction here is remarkably consistent through my samples. The Stuffy Talker uses far fewer finite verbs (6 per cent of total words) than do the Sweet and the Tough Talker (both 11 per cent). This is part of the general distinction that pervades these figures, between formal-written language and informal-conversational language. We mentioned in Chapter 3 the classic Tough Talker's unwillingness to subordinate, an unwillingness that makes for simple sentence structures and a high proportion of finite verbs. The Stuffy Talker, on the other hand, qualifies his remarks with much subordination and modification, so that in officialese we find the verb followed by a whole series of constructions added to prevent misunderstanding. "Advice *has been requested* concerning the deductibility for Federal income tax purposes of research expenses, including traveling expenses, incurred by college and university professors in their capacity as educators." (One verb in a 29-word sentence.)

My figures are too tiny, but a word can be said in passing about base verbs—that is, uninflected verb forms used without any auxiliary. These are far more common in Sweet Talk than in either of the other two styles, partly because of Sweet Talk's fondness for the second person, including imperatives. "Wait till you taste these new dinners." Two base verbs in a 7-word sentence.

A note may also be added about the modal auxiliaries—may, might, can, could, would, should, must, and ought. These words express some kind of attitude (it has been called "emotional") toward the action that the verb names. Again Sweet Talk is well in the lead, though the figures are minute. In Tough Talk the characteristic verb form seems to be a simple inflection: this happened and that happened. Stuffy Talk, fond of elaborate qualification, takes more advantage of the subtleties offered by auxiliaries. But all this is guesswork needing to be tested.

6. *What proportion of the finitive verbs are forms of* to be?

Here I am not considering *to be* as an auxiliary. The Tough Talker in my samples is fonder of this verb than the others are; the figures are 36 per cent against 25 per cent for Sweet Talk and 17 per cent for Stuffy Talk. I submit that this is part of the urge for naming mentioned in Chapters 3 and 4, a liking for a particular sentence pattern of the "this-is-that" construction.[2] In some of its appearances, it can come close to omniscience, as in *Time's* "The scenes in Birmingham were unforgettable." The six Tough Talkers are not very consistent about this, but I include the point for what it may be worth.

7. *What proportion of the finitive verbs are in the passive voice?*

There is no problem here. Stuffy Talkers use the passive voice, others do not. It is a sure-fire technique for avoiding personal responsibility for one's statements, and when the Revenue Service winds up for a decision, it does not say "we conclude . . ." but "it is held that. . . ." By whom?

Slightly over one-quarter (26 per cent) of the finite verbs in my samples of Stuffy Talk are in the passive. The figure for Tough Talk is 4 per cent and for Sweet Talk 2 per cent. In all Stuffy Talkers except the marginal "Teaching Literature" the writers use a passive at least once in every six verbs.

D. QUESTIONS ABOUT MODIFICATION

This is another area I am unashamedly skimming. Phrases and clauses used as modifiers of various kinds are unmentioned. What, for instance, is the effect of a series of piled-up prepositional phrases? Are they always Stuffy? How does frequency of adverbs contribute to tone? Etc.

8. *What proportion of the total words are true adjectives?*

As we saw in Chapter 6, one way to distinguish a "true" adjective is to ask whether it can be rendered in the comparative degree, either by inflection or the use of a function word. (*Fine, finer; interesting, more interesting.*) Or whether it can be translated into a sentence with this construction: The interesting story is very interesting. In these ways an adjective can be differentiated from a noun adjunct construction (like *income tax*). One cannot say (and call it English) "The income tax is very income," nor can one say "the tax is more income," "the tax is incomer."

Modification, as we also said in Chapter 6, is the bread-and-butter of the adman, and we find accordingly 11 per cent of the total wordage in Sweet Talk composed of adjectives as defined above. The Stuffy Talkers are not far behind, at 8 per cent. Adjectives in Tough Talk come to 6 per cent. All six Tough Talkers are sparing with adjectives, less than one word out of ten in each passage being an adjective as here defined. Almost all the Sweet Talkers use adjectives at least once out of every ten words, and some of them plaster their nouns liberally with this kind of modification. "All brand-new in a pleasing new size . . . wide-open spaces . . . refreshing new styling . . . a huge 27-foot trunk . . ." and so on.

In comparisons and superlatives of adjectives, we may note in passing that Sweet Talk is again far in the lead, though the figures are small. There are only 2 in Tough Talk, 6 in Stuffy Talk, 19 in Sweet Talk. Things being sold are better, newest, finest. In all styles the inflected comparisons are in excess of those adjectives that require function words (as in Smoking's *less extensive*). This is curious in the light of Fries' observation, a quarter century ago, that the ratio of inflected and noninflected comparisons in Standard English was about half and half.[3]

9. *How many adjectives are themselves modified by intensifiers or other adverbs?*

Here we are looking for a particular example of modification that might be called excessive—that is, when the adjective modifying a noun is itself modified by an adverb. Often this adverb serves only to pad up the force of the adjective (*just right, perfectly adequate*), and can be called an "intensifier." (See Chapter 6.) I do not include *more* used strictly as a comparative (but I do count it in the expression *one of the more maddening insolences of criticism,* where it seems to act simply as an intensifier). I do not count *so* in a *so . . . that* construction (*the pressure was so high that . . .*), but do count it when used as an intensifier only (*so many people do not know how to read*).

The figures are tiny but interesting. There are 4 such expressions in Tough Talk, 3 in Stuffy Talk, 12 in Sweet Talk. *More maddening* and *perturbingly moving* occur in "Unrequired Reading," while the ads offer the following: *otherwise well ordered, perfectly adequate, specially and deliciously different* (a double entry), *just right, deliciously smooth, unusually good, homemade good, so much better, all brand-new.*

I surmise that the presence of this construction about once every hundred words is a characteristic of Sweet Talk, but not of the others.

10. *What proportion of the total words are noun adjuncts?*

The particular inventiveness which characterizes many noun adjuncts in advertising was discussed in Chapter 6. Made-up phrases like *Foodarama living* and *stretch-out interior room* are characteristic of Sweet Talk. Every example in our Sweet Talk collection (except Ad #3) contains at least two noun adjunct constructions, and many of them are of the nonce sort I have illustrated. But the frequency (not the inventiveness) of noun adjuncts in Stuffy Talk is even higher—there are 55 such constructions, over 5 per cent of the total words. The Revenue passage is illustrative: *income tax purposes, research expenses, traveling expenses, college and university professors*. The Tough Talkers, on the other hand, employ only ten noun adjuncts throughout, three of them in *Time*'s journalism. The others are conventional expressions like *fruit trees, dirt shoulder, world brotherhood*.

The explanation here is complex. In Sweet Talk, I have argued, the passion for noun adjuncts is part of the passion for naming, and a substitute for Tough Talk's abundance of *to be* and the "this-is-that" sentence pattern. In Stuffy Talk, the multiple names have already been coined, and they roll off the stuffy tongue in great official bundles, like *the College Entrance Examination Board's Scholastic Aptitude and Achievement Test* ("Admissions").[4] But Tough Talk, often, aspires to speech patterns like those of Fries' Vulgar English samples in his famous study. More than once Fries has occasion to point out the relative conservatism, linguistically, of his Vulgar writers; they cling to old forms when others have given them up. Similarly they fail to leap on to current linguistic bandwagons, notably the noun-adjunct bandwagon. Fries found noun adjuncts in his so-called Standard writers four times as frequent as in his Vulgar.[5] This is almost exactly the relation between my Sweet and Stuffy Talkers as against my Tough Talkers.

One would at first surmise that the adman's language aspires to Vulgarity too, but this is only partly true. Unlike Vulgar English and unlike the conversation of most people, Sweet Talk can be daring and resourceful in inventing new forms of expression. This daring is most conspicuous, I think, in the use of the noun adjunct.

Associated with noun adjuncts is the question of the inflected genitive, though my figures are too tiny for more than speculation. The substitution of the inflected genitive for the phrase with *of* is another of *Time*'s contributions to modern journalistic style, exemplified in our materials by the expression *Birmingham's Negroes* in place of the more orthodox *the Negroes of Birmingham*. But that is the only example of an inflected genitive in all of Tough Talk, while the only one in Stuffy Talk is *the College Board's . . . Tests* ("Admissions"). In Sweet Talk, with its desire to give things names, perhaps also to add that crisp authority conveyed by the mannerisms of Timestyle, there are nine instances of the inflected genitive. *Chase Manhattan's dish of tea. The world's best-selling scotch. Foodarama's supermarket selection.* (Inflected genitive and noun adjunct all in one phrase.) All examples are not from adwriters, either; there are three in "Unrequired Reading," though they lack the commercial touch of the ones I mentioned.

E. QUESTIONS ABOUT SUBORDINATION

In this section I consider mostly the sheer bulk of the clauses in my three styles, but there are several other matters with respect to clauses that are too tentative, in the present state of my samples, to put forward as more than faintly suggestive. For one thing there appear to be, in Tough Talk, somewhat more adverbial clauses modifying whole sentences than in the other two. Part of Tough Talk's reluctance to modify nouns specifically? Part of Tough Talk's reluctance to assume a role of omniscience, preferring to modify or qualify an entire statement? This last possibility is encouraged by the discovery of 6 *if* clauses in Tough Talk, only 2 in Sweet Talk and one in Stuffy Talk.

Sweet Talk seems slightly partial to the adjective clause, as we might expect. There is furthermore a particular form of noun-modifying clause in which the function word, or "includer" (usually *that*), can be omitted. Examples are *the dust they raised* (Frederic Henry) and *the way you like it* (Ad #6). Jespersen calls this a contact clause, and indicates it has a long and distinguished history.[6] Fries found its use more frequent in Vulgar English than in Standard. Associated as it therefore is with informal discourse, we find two examples in Tough Talk, three in Sweet Talk, none in Stuffy Talk.

11. *What is the average length of the included clauses?*

An included clause is the modern linguist's term, or one of his terms, for what we used to call a subordinate or dependent clause. One immediately startling fact about my samples is that the sheer number of such clauses is higher in Tough and Sweet Talk than in Stuffy Talk. There are 32 clauses each in the first two, only 17 in Stuffy Talk. The length of the characteristic clauses in the styles is, however, very different: an average of 8 words each in Tough Talk, 7 words each in Sweet Talk, 18 in Stuffy Talk. Of the Tough Talkers, only Jack Burden's windiness exceeds an average 10 words per included clause. All Stuffy Talkers average above this figure, and one ("Revenue") averages 25 words per clause.

12. *What proportion of the total passage is inside such clauses?*

It follows from the above that Stuffy Talk, in spite of having fewer clauses by a good deal, nevertheless displays a larger proportion of its total text inside included clauses. The figures are 24 per cent. for Tough Talk, 23 per cent for Sweet Talk, 32 per cent for Stuffy Talk. Among the last-named, the extreme is "Teaching Literature," half of whose total text appears inside clauses. But this is apparently not always a critical matter, for both "Smoking" and "Admissions" are fairly low in total wordage of clauses.

Insofar as clauses relate to tone, it is clear that frequency of subordination is not much help. Tough and Sweet Talkers use the included clause generously. They do, however, use shorter clauses, and at least in most cases they place a smaller fraction of their discourse within clauses than the Stuffy Talkers do.

13. *How frequently are subject and main verb separated by intervening subordinate structures? How long are these interruptions?*

Much depends not only on the *number* and the *length* of subordinate structures, but also on their *placing* in the sentence. One can place one's included clause, for example, ahead of one's subject-verb, in what is called a left-branching construction, or behind one's subject-verb, in a right-branching construction. Consider examples from our Dickens-Bellow contrast of Chapter 5. "Whether I shall turn out to be the hero of my own life . . . these pages must show," says David Copperfield, and we sense, as we dive into that complicated clause at the *beginning* of the book, that here is a stylist who already knows how his sentence (maybe his book too?) is going to end. If he is already foisting off on us dependent structures, then he must know what they're going to be dependent *on*. A well-ordered mind. Not so Augie, of course: "My parents were not much to me, though I cared for my mother." As an afterthought, a qualification, the clause appears behind the subject-verb and supports the casual voice we observed in Chapter 5.

No doubt an analysis of left-branching and right-branching subordination would turn up something with respect to my styles, but I intend to confine myself here to still a third *placing* of subordinate structures—*between* subject and main verb. I am counting, simply enough, all the words that intervene in our passages between a subject and its verb, with the suspicion that what is called "self-embedding" constructions may be a symptom of the Stuffy Talker.[7]

The figures are heartening—and if they were not, I need scarcely say, you would not be hearing about them. The Tough Talkers interrupt their subjects and verbs very little, Jack Burden and Augie March not at all. Out of a total of 102 subject-verb combinations, there are only 24 interrupting words. Sweet Talk is almost as sparing in its separations of subject and verb, 96 combinations and 36 intervening words. (A third of them occurs in the professorial "Unrequired Reading.") In Stuffy Talk we have just the contrary picture: in 57 subject-verb combinations, there are 182 words in "self-embedding" positions. One of the flashier examples occurs in "Smoking": "The *risk* of developing cancer of the lung for the combined group of pipe smokers, cigar smokers, and pipe and cigar smokers *is* . . ."

I conclude that if the total number of "self-embedding" words is less than half the total number of subject-verb structures, the passage is in this respect safely within the Tough-Sweet categories. On the other hand, twice as many interrupting words as there are subject-verb combinations suggests the pontifical voice of the Stuffy Talker.

F. OTHER EFFECTS OF TONE

14. *What is the frequency of the determiner* the?

The significance of using *the* liberally was discussed at length in Chapter 3, where I argued its function as an *implied* expression of intimacy. If I began a story by saying "The long street down the hill . . . ," I imply that you and I have some relationship already in operation, and that you know me well enough to be aware what street and hill I'm talking about. This intimacy is almost always fictitious, of course, whether in "fiction" or elsewhere.

There are 97 appearances of *the* in Tough Talk, 39 in Sweet Talk, 65 in Stuffy Talk. In this case it is Stuffy Talk that is in the middle, and 6-7 per cent may represent the approximate frequency of *the* in contemporary American prose. (The huge "Standard Corpus" just assembled at Brown University, however, suggests a frequency as high as 7.8%.) At the present state of our findings, the Tough Talker seems to be characteristically above this average figure, and the Sweet Talker below it.

15. *Are there any sentences without subjects, or without verbs, or without either? Are there any contractions?*

Sweet Talk's directly expressed intimacy of tone can obviously make good use of contractions common to colloquial speech. Of these there are 24 in my samples, appearing in every passage except "Unrequired Reading." Tough Talk, as we know, also echoes speech patterns, in its different way; in my samples there are 16 contractions, half of them in Jack Burden. There are no contractions in Stuffy Talk.

Even more telling may be the behavior of the three styles with respect to what are called "sentence fragments." These are groups of words punctuated as sentences, but lacking a subject or a verb or both. Ad #5 is a goldmine of fragments. *Not me, darling. Itchy skin? At any drug or cosmetic counter.* There are 20 of these constructions scattered through 5 of the ads. Example lacking the verb: *Every man his own connoisseur* (Ad #3). Lacking the subject: *Gives my skin precious moisture* (Ad #5). Lacking both: *And a wide range of new decorator colors* (Ad #8).

In Tough Talk there are two verbless sentences, both from Earl Horter, and one subjectless sentence, from Jack Burden. There are no such sentences in Stuffy Talk.

16. *How many occurrences are there of these marks of punctuation: italics, parentheses, dashes, question marks, exclamation points?*

The totals of our three styles in respect to these marks of punctuation are as follows: Tough Talk, one question, 2 dashes. Sweet Talk: 7 italics (or boldface or capitals), 4 sets of parentheses, 9 dashes, 8 questions, 5 exclamations. Stuffy Talk: 2 sets of parentheses (both in "Smoking").

Italics. All five devices are used to effect a close relation with the assumed reader (among other functions they may have), and the Sweet Talker accordingly makes generous use of all of them. I first consider italics. As we have seen repeatedly, the Sweet Talker's problem is to simulate as convincingly as he can the voice of intimate conversation. In this effort he is considerably handicapped by the shortcomings of our writing system, which is simply not equipped to express the sounds that a voicebox makes. (The linguist counts in actual speech eight "phonemes" of stress and pitch alone, and these are conspicuously inexpressible by any written symbol, or "grapheme.") It is what the physical voice does *while* it is pronouncing syllables—its undulations of pitch and stress—that the written language particularly disregards. These, the so-called "supersegmental phonemes," can be graphically expressed only by differences in the appearance of the typeface, differences in the spacing or color or size or shape. In this essay I am considering only very obvious cases of conventional supersegmental emphasis, through italics, boldface type, or a spelling in capital letters. Of these there are seven in my Sweet samples. But I emphasize that in the adwriter's performance there is tremendous pictorial razzle-dazzle which I am not measuring here, but which contributes greatly to our comprehension of the speaking voice addressing us. The artistry that goes into layout, color, and so on is highly important to the whole effect.[8] To mention one simple example, variation in line length to bring words and phrases into prominence, as in poetry, is simply not available to the ordinary prose-writer, whose line endings are controlled by the typographer. Such a technique may be admired in Ad #5, where I have attempted to reproduce the appearance of the actual ad.

Parentheses. Sets of parentheses, especially when they occur repeatedly, are a clear call for intimacy. At their most extreme they are like a whisper, a sotto-voce uttered behind the hand. You and I share a joke, or a revelation, or a secret, and nobody else can hear. Sets of parentheses provide another way, crude though it is, by which the Sweet Talker can indicate variation in his tone of voice. (Three examples in Ad #5.) When used more sparingly, parentheses serve a conventional function in Tough and Stuffy Talk as well, as the two examples in "Smoking" will illustrate.

Dashes. The liberal use of the dash gives an effect of breathlessness—literally a characteristic of an actual speaking voice. Women who punctuate letters entirely with this mark are presumably endeavoring to capture the sound of an intense human voice in action. Furthermore, relations between parts of a sentence connected by dashes remain logically in the air, another characteristic of our elliptical and loose syntax in conversation. I take it that, other things being equal, the more dashes I use, the closer I am to you and the more realistically I echo the sound of intimate discourse.

Questions. When you ask a question, you expect an answer,

or you pretend you do. More than any other mark of end-punctuation the question mark engages the assumed reader directly. I'm asking *you*—even though you may know I'm about to provide the answer myself. There are seven questions in Ad #5, another in #3. A single question, a very rhetorical one, appears in Tough Talk, at the end of Earl Horter. There are no questions in Stuffy Talk, for the Stuffy Talker hardly knows his reader exists.

Exclamations. The exclamation mark appeals to the reader by laying stress on the speaker's own excitement. Now hear this!!! It is a primitive instrument, when you consider the enormous variations of which the human voice is capable in an enthusiastic state. Still, the adwriter does what he can, and we have 5 instances of the exclamation mark in Sweet Talk, none in Tough Talk or in Stuffy.

And now the style machine. I summarize below the answers to my fifteen questions, as they are worked out in averages for the thousand words of each style. Then I propose criteria for each question, by means of which any passage of prose might be tested to see whether it qualifies, in that particular category, as Tough, Sweet, or Stuffy. After that I try the machine at measuring individually the various passages we have been examining in this study. Finally, in a Style Sampler (Appendix B), I try measuring other prose passages, to see whether the machine can provide a numerical score that might be taken as a reasonable translation of our impression of a voice.

FACTS ABOUT THE PASSAGES

	Tough	Sweet	Stuffy
1. What is the proportion of monosyllables in the passage?	78%	68%	56%

2. What is the proportion of words of more than 2 syllables?	5%	12%	24%
3. How many first-person and second-person pronouns does the passage contain?	13 1st 21 2nd	12 1st 42 2nd	2 1st 0 2nd
4. Are the subjects of finite verbs neuter nouns, or nouns referring to people?	52 N 72 P	45 N 70 P	51 N 14 P
5. What is the proportion of finite verbs to total words?	11%	11%	6%
6. What proportion of finite verbs are forms of *to be*?	36%	25%	17%
7. What proportion of verbs are in the passive voice?	4%	2%	26%
8. What proportion of words are true adjectives?	6%	11%	8%
9. How many adjectives are modified by adverbs?	4	13	5
10. What proportion of words are noun adjuncts?	1%	4%	5%
11. What is the average length of included clauses?	8 wds	7 wds	18 wds
12. What proportion of total passage is inside such clauses?	24%	23%	32%
13. How many words separate subject and verb?	24 wds	36 wds	182 wds
14. How frequent is the determiner *the*?	97	39	65
15. How many fragments? How many contractions?	2 fr 16 cn	20 fr 24 cn	0 fr 0 cn
16. How many parentheses, italics, dashes, question marks, exclamation points?	0 P 0 I 2 D 1 Q 0 E	4 P 7 I 9 D 8 Q 5 E	2 P 0 I 0 D 0 Q 0 E

THE STYLE MACHINE

CRITERIA FOR MEASURING STYLE

	Tough	*Sweet*	*Stuffy*
1. Monosyllables	over 70%	61-70%	60% or less
2. Words of 3 syllables and more	under 10%	10-19%	20% or more
3. 1st and 2nd person pronouns	1 *I* or *we* per 100 words	2 *you* per 100 words	no 1st or 2nd person pronouns
4. Subjects: neuters vs. people	½ or more people	½ or more people	⅔ or more neuters
5. Finite verbs	over 10%	over 10%	under 10%
6. *To be* forms as finite verbs	over ⅓ of verbs	under ¼	under ¼
7. Passives	less than 1 in 20 verbs	none	more than 1 in 5 verbs
8. True adjectives	under 10%	over 10%	over 8%
9. Adjectives modified	fewer than 1 per 100 words	1 or more	fewer than 1
10. Noun adjuncts	under 2%	2% or more	4% or more
11. Average length of clauses	10 words or less	10 words or less	more than 10 words
12. Clauses, proportion of total words	¼ or less	⅓ or less	over 40%
13. "Embedded" words	less than ½ S/V combinations	less than half	more than twice
14. *The*	8% or more	under 6%	6-7%
15. Contractions and fragments	1 or more per 100 words	2 or more	none
16. Parentheses & other punctuation	none	2 or more per 100 words	none

Now here are some results, based on these criteria, for the six passages I have labeled Tough in this study:

TOUGH TALKERS

	Tough	Sweet	Stuffy
"Private World" (Chapter 2)	11	5	4
Frederic Henry (Chapter 3)	13	4	4
Time magazine (Chapter 4)	11	5	3
Augie March (Chapter 5)	15	7	2
Jack Burden (Chapter 5)	12	5	5
Earl Horter (Chapter 5)	13	8	0

All our Tough Talkers emerge in two figures for Toughness, which is encouraging. Small differences in the present state of this machine will have to be disregarded: why should Augie rate "two points tougher" than Frederic Henry? No reason. On the other hand, Earl Horter's high rating in Sweetness does support our feeling that Earl seemed a good deal friendlier than, say, Frederic Henry, and was by no means so sternly "a hard man in a violent world." The fact that Jack Burden, he of the elaborate clauses and the graduate education, rates highest in Stuffiness also seems to me reassuring.

SWEET TALKERS

	Tough	Sweet	Stuffy
"Unrequired Reading" (Chapter 2)	5	10	4
Ad #1 (Chase Bank) (Chapter 6)	7	12	4
Ad #2 (Newsweek)	9	13	3
Ad #3 (Johnny Walker)	6	12	2
Ad #4 (Bell Telephone)	5	12	3
Ad #5 (Sardo)	10	12	1
Ad #6 (Kraft)	8	12	5
Ad #7 (Kelvinator)	6	13	3
Ad #8 (Chevrolet)	6	12	2

Again we see all Sweet Talkers emerging in two figures for Sweetness, but here there are some embarrassing high scores in Toughness as well. The lovely lady of the Sardo ad is the hardest to explain away; she scores almost as high in Toughness as she does in Sweetness. Why? Here is one of the major bugs in my machine, in its present lamentable condition: almost any very simple prose, with little modification and little subordination, will show up fairly Tough. Pulp-magazine stories, for example. It is evidently possible to write Sweetly while using many of the Tough Talker's rhetorical habits, at least as I have defined them. How to distinguish between simple rhetoric that is Tough and simple rhetoric that is just simpleminded?

STUFFY TALKERS

	Tough	Sweet	Stuffy
"Teaching Literature" (Chapter 2)	3	3	12
"Smoking" (2 passages) (Chapter 7)	1	4	13
"Revenue" (Chapter 7)	2	2	16
"Admissions" (Chapter 7)	3	3	13

These figures are by far the most satisfactory, since Stuffiness is the easiest style to define and isolate. Note that none of our Stuffy Talkers rates higher than 3 in Toughness or higher than 4 in Sweetness. We also have here our only example of Pure Style, in the rating of 16 for the Revenue Service document. That passage, I conclude, embodies the Unadulterated Stuffy Voice Incarnate.

It may be illuminating now to go back to those four passages about the teaching of reading, from Chapter 2. We identified there a sample of Tough Talk, one of Sweet Talk, one of Stuffy Talk, and one (T. S. Eliot) that seemed not to fall into any of these descriptions. Those impressions, translated into numbers through the good offices of the style machine, look like this:

	Tough	Sweet	Stuffy
"Private World" (Tough)	11	5	4
"Unrequired Reading" (Sweet)	5	10	4
"Teaching Literature" (Stuffy)	3	3	12
Eliot (mixed)	6	6	4

From this small exhibit it is tempting to surmise that most decent expository prose avoids all three of my extreme styles, following a *via media* of good sense and a golden mean. While there may be some practical truth to that guess, there are plenty of exceptions, as anyone can discover by trying out these tests at random, or by glancing at the Style Sampler in Appendix B.

In similar fashion, we may take a last look at those three pieces of journalism discussed in Chapter 4, on the same "event" (the Birmingham race riots). One (*New York Times*) I called an example of "straight," detached reporting; one (*Herald Tribune*) purported to avoid dullness by adopting some omniscient assumptions of the novelist; and one (*Time*) combined omniscience with the rhetoric and general personality of the Tough Talker. Run through the machine, these passages emerge with these figures:

	Tough	Sweet	Stuffy
New York Times	6	5	10
Herald Tribune	6	6	10
Time	11	5	3

We note with these figures some additional facts about our experience of reading that the machine simply doesn't measure. The styles of the *Times* and *Tribune* appear virtually identical; the machine cannot detect "dishonesty." It can, however, detect the Tough Talker's rhetoric, to the degree that *Time* rates high in that column. The high rating in Stuffiness for both newspapers may be a reminder of how hard it is to write a report that is "detached" without at the same time writing one that is "irresponsible" in the manner of the Stuffy Talker. In fact this dilemma may stand at the heart of newswriting. For all its pretension to liveliness, the *Tribune* does not seem to have solved the problem, at least in this passage and this measurement. See, however, Sample #10 in the Style Sampler.

APPENDIX B

A STYLE SAMPLER
Mostly Tough, Mostly Sweet, Mostly Stuffy, and Some Mixtures

"The style machine is just a piece of paper."
—Remark by John S. Gibson, age 6

What follows is a miscellany of very short passages, usually introductory passages, which have been submitted to the style machine and rated for Toughness-Sweetness-Stuffiness. Part of my point is to stress the fact that these three styles are not confined to particular genres of writing. There are no modern novels among the passages rated Mostly Tough, no ads among those rated Mostly Sweet, and only one example of committee writing (juvenile at that) in the Mostly Stuffy division. My Mixed samples include authors as disparate as Jack Kerouac and Abraham Lincoln, suggesting surely that anything can be Mixed, in however different proportions, and that the machine's value judgments are rather on the crude side. But there are nevertheless pretensions of value in the operations of this primitive gadget. Insofar as the machine can sometimes detect a Tough Talker going Sweet, and insofar as it can identify excesses of both Sweetness and Stuffiness, it should offer some help in documenting our intuitive impressions.

The reader is invited to try the machine on his own writing, if he can endure the twenty minutes of dreary arthimetic necessary. I have tried it on mine with results not altogether reassuring. Mixed, but a little too Sweet for comfort. I am tempted to rewrite this essay forthwith, cutting down the modifiers, tightening the punctuation, removing the contractions. But I let it stand, after all, an example of Imperfect Style. A poor thing but my own.

CONTENTS OF THE STYLE SAMPLER

MOSTLY TOUGH

1. Speech by Winston Churchill ("We shall go on. . . .")
2. Marvell's "Coy Mistress"
3. Gertrude Stein
4. An editorial in *Sports Illustrated*
5. A letter from Raymond Chandler

MOSTLY SWEET

6. A novel by Hayden Carruth
7. An article in *Glamour* magazine
8. United Air Lines instructions for emergency escape
9. An article in the New York *Journal American*
10. Tom Wolfe in the *Herald Tribune*

MOSTLY STUFFY

11. Jerome Bruner
12. Paul Tillich
13. Newsletter from the New Jersey State Division on Aging

14. Article in PMLA
15. Resolution of the Christian Association, Swarthmore College

MIXED

16. William James
17. Henry James
18. Erich Fromm
19. J. B. Conant
20. A letter from Merrill Lynch
21. William Faulkner
22. Jack Kerouac
23. Paul Goodman
24. The Declaration of Independence
25. The Gettysburg Address

Sample #1—Mostly Tough

We shall go on to the end, we shall fight in France, we shall fight on the seas and oceans, we shall fight with growing confidence and growing strength in the air, we shall defend our Island, whatever the cost may be, we shall fight on the beaches, we shall fight on the landing grounds, we shall fight in the fields and in the streets, we shall fight in the hills; we shall never surrender, and even if, which I do not for a moment believe, this Island or a large part of it were subjugated and starving, then our Empire beyond the seas, armed and guarded by the British Fleet, would carry on the struggle, until, in God's good time, the New World, with all its power and might, steps forth to the rescue and the liberation of the old.

—Winston Churchill

Score: 10—4—5

Comment: This famous passage by a stylist we tend to classify with the late Victorians turns out not to be Stuffy after all, at least according to the machine. Churchill was certainly a hard man who had been around, and in this sentence, anyway, his rhetoric supports the hardness. The machine does not take note of the repeated parallel structures in the passage, and these may add a literary formality not usually associated with Tough Talk. Nevertheless, in brevity of diction, spareness of modification, heavy reliance on the definite article, Churchill here echoes patterns we have identified as Tough.

Sample #2—Mostly Tough

Had we but world enough, and time, this coyness, Lady, were no crime. We would sit down and think which way to walk and pass our long love's day. Thou by the Indian Ganges' side shouldst rubies find; I by the tide of Humber would complain. I would love you ten years before the Flood, and you should, if you please, refuse till the conversion of the Jews. My vegetable love should grow vaster than empires, and more slow; an hundred years should go to praise thine eyes and on thy forehead gaze; two hundred to adore each breast, but thirty thousand to the rest; an age at least to every part, and the last age should show your heart.

—Marvell, "To His Coy Mistress"

Score: 12—6—5

Comment: Poetry is Tougher than prose; the speaker in a good poem is almost by definition a hard man who has been around in a violent world, who is concerned with himself more than with the reader, and who is sparing with modification, subordination, and fancy vocabulary. Marvell's lover measures Tougher than any other voice in this collection of samples.

Sample #3—Mostly Tough

What is poetry and if you know what poetry is what is prose.

There is no use in telling more than you know, no not even if you do not know it.

But do you do you know what prose is and do you know what poetry is.

I have said that the words in plays written in poetry are more lively than the same words written by the same poet in other kinds of poetry. It undoubtedly was true of Shakespeare, it is inevitably true of everybody. That is one thing to think about. I said that the words in a play written in prose are not as lively words as the words written in other prose by the same writer.

                    —Gertrude Stein, "Poetry and Grammar"

Score: 10—6—4

Comment: Readers may feel the machine particularly inadequate with prose like this. Some works for children might score as high in Toughness, even when we feel the voice as something quite other than Tough. These sentences contain an extraordinary number of finite verbs, 18 of them, and 11 of these are forms of *to be*. Miss Stein tells us, or asks us, what something *is*. On the other hand there are gestures toward formality: fairly lengthy clauses, a refusal to use contractions even though the reader is addressed directly and idiomatically.

Sample #4—Mostly Tough

A week or so ago, when we had a warmish day between blustery snowstorms here in the East, I caught a glimpse of the first sure sign of spring. A couple of 12-year-old kids had baseball gloves on and were playing catch—in February. Of course, it was colder than they had assumed and they didn't keep it up very long, but there it was: baseball was back.

Despite such eager kids, the season really begins for me each year when we print our first baseball cover—as we do this week. Opening Day is still six weeks off, but our cover says that right now the ballplayers are in the sun country, and the training camps are moving into high gear. And the feeling is good.

—"Letter from the Publisher" in *Sports Illustrated*, February 1966

Score: 10—7—4

Comment: The loose-talking, or Luce-talking, voice here, so familiar in journalism, derives from the supersimplicity of the Tough novelist, but is going Sweet. Sentimentality, always a danger in Tough Talk, is here right on the surface, as in that last sentence. Perhaps we can imagine a Hemingway dealing satisfactorily with this little scene, but it takes more skill than is evident in this Letter from this Publisher.

Sample #5—Mostly Tough

I sit up half the night playing records when I have the blues and can't get drunk enough to feel sleepy. My nights are pretty awful. And they don't get any better. I've been alone since Saturday morning except for Mabel the Marble, my Pennsylvania Dutch cook and housekeeper. She has a lot of fine qualities but she is not much company. Perhaps when I get away from this house and all its memories I can settle down to do some writing. And then again I may just be homesick, and to be homesick for a home you haven't got is rather poignant.

Tomorrow is or would have been our thirty-first wedding anniversary. I'm going to fill the house with red roses and have a friend in to drink champagne, which we always did. A useless and probably foolish gesture because my lost love is utterly lost and I have no belief in any after life. But just the same I shall do it. All us tough guys are hopeless sentimentalists at heart.

 —From a letter by Raymond Chandler, February 7, 1955.
 Raymond Chandler Speaking (Boston, 1962).

Score: 10—9—1

Comment: This passage by one of the supposed daddies of Tough Talk might better be included in my Mixed classification, but it remains a nice example of the Tough voice in decay, oozing away into Sweetness, and self-conscious about it at that. All us tough guys are hopeless sentimentalists at heart. Here the most outstanding characteristics of Sweetness, as identified by the machine, are the adjectives and the modifiers of adjectives. *Pretty awful, rather poignant, probably foolish, utterly lost.* There is no direct appeal to the reader (*you*), but the mushiness of the self-pity is certainly supported by the mushiness of the rhetoric. (The book's jacket advertises, "the master stylist . . . at ease in the wisest and toughest of letters.") Compare Sample #6.

Sample #6—Mostly Sweet

Forgive me for being so late. I always have the devil's own time getting started, if you want to know the truth. You're aware of the type? Continually putting things off? I think of people like Agassiz or Fangio or Goethe, the big doers, guys with a list of accomplishments five yards long, and it's not their genius that depresses me so much, though God knows I feel the lack of it—usually anyway; then sometimes I get hopped up on an idea for a poem and I wonder what genius is anyway, who's got it, whether anybody's got it, etc.—but as I say, it's not the ability of great men that depresses me so much as their goddamned readiness to begin.

—Hayden Carruth, *Appendik A* (1963)

Score: 9—10—0

Comment: This opening paragraph of a modern novel is an extreme example of the Tough voice gone Sweet, as discussed in Chapter 4. Very unbuttoned, and willing to address the reader directly in the most conversational way. The relation of this sloppy narrator to his assumed author poses a problem for the sympathetic reader. This fellow has many of Augie March's rhetorical habits, but he is a weaker character, and the weakness is to some degree indicated by the machine's score.

The overt self-consciousness about language that we mentioned in Hemingway, Salinger, and others is here almost parodied. Chapter 2 of Carruth's novel begins: "The tone of that first chapter is uncertain, I know; timorous, hesitant, stumbling, a touch forlorn—in the conventional manner of ingratiation. Never mind; I'll go back to it and fix it later . . ." The question is, of course: who is the "I" who did, or didn't, go back and fix it later?

Sample #7—*Mostly Sweet*

At eighteen, money starts coming in in a greater variety of ways—a bigger allowance, a job, more profitable part-time projects. After years of frugality, you may be surprised to find money falling into your lap in this seemingly undeserved profusion, and to find yourself suddenly able to afford possessions you'd never dreamed of owning. But, at eighteen, your income's likely to be uncertain. A sudden windfall can open up vistas for the most adult extravagances—then, zoop, down to ten dollars, you're ten years old again, and nonindependent as a child.

You can learn, however, from your fluctuating finances.

—From *Glamour* magazine, September 1965

Score: 5—12—3

Comment: Monosyllables in this passage come to only 58 per cent, which is close to the average of Stuffy Talk! Is such diction supposed to demonstrate rhetorically "the most adult extravagances"? An affected ritziness to flatter the eighteen-year-old reader? In any case, the passage is in other respects decidedly Sweet, with an interesting rejection of the determiner. There is only one *the* in the entire selection.

Sample #8—Mostly Sweet

FOR YOUR SAFETY. Know how to move out of this airplane fast. There is fire-danger any time a landing is other than normal—particularly when the airplane structure is damaged.

Below is a floor plan of the plane you are in. Familiarize yourself with the location of the exits. Note particularly the exits nearest you. Study how they are opened and also the protective position you should assume during an emergency landing. When leaving, move to the exits immediately. Do not go back for coats, purses, or other personal items.

A WORD ABOUT YOUR SEAT BELT. Rough air (turbulence) at high altitudes, though infrequent, can be severe. When the seat belt sign is lighted in-flight, please comply with the sign to prevent possible injury. Seasoned air travelers usually leave their seat belts fastened all the time and pull them up snug whenever the seat belt sign is lighted.

—United Air Lines, instructions to passengers

Score: 6—11—5

Comment: It may be comforting to timid flyers to find that even the disaster plans are couched in rhetoric close to that of advertising. Plenty of second-person appeal, including imperative verbs, and very simple sentence patterns. There is perceptible Stuffiness here too, however, as befits a solemn statement from a great organization: witness the symptomatic noun adjuncts (*seat belt sign, air travelers*, etc.) and the generous use of passive verbs.

Sample #9—Mostly Sweet

Your Hands can be one of the most beautiful things about you. Make them "happy" by giving them the extra-special care they deserve. To eliminate nail problems, carefully massage cream (special nail cream is best) into your cuticles every day and get into the habit of pushing cuticles back gently with a towel whenever your hands are damp.

Did you know that you can actually change the shape of your fingers? Pinch the tips lightly each time you clean your hands, especially after applying lotion, to insure gracefully tapered fingers.

Religiously set aside some time for a once-a-week manicure. There's nothing like soft, feminine hands with beautifully cared-for nails to set male hearts aflutter.

—Article in the New York *Journal American*,
March 19, 1966

Score: 7—14—0

Comment: This is just about as Sweet as you can get, dearie. The passage qualifies in every possible category except two. Note that, like all Sweet Talk, it does *not* employ the stripped-down monosyllabic vocabulary of Toughness. Modification is very generous, and the presence of eight *-ly* adverbs seems to

me particularly significant, though the machine as now constructed does not take account of them.

Sample #10—Mostly Sweet

What if he's right What . . . if . . . he . . .
is . . . right W-h-a-t i-f h-e i-s r-i-g-h-t

W	IF	R	
H	HE	I	
A	IS	G	?
T		H	
		T	

There are currently hundreds of studs of the business world,
breakfast food package designers, television network Creative
Department vice-presidents, advertising "media reps," light-
ing fixture fortune heirs, smiley patent lawyers, industrial
spies, we-need-Vision board chairmen, all sorts of business
studs who are all wondering if this man, Marshall McLuhan
. . . is right. McLuhan is a 54-year-old Canadian professor. He
sits in a little office off on the edge of the University of
Toronto that looks like the receiving bin of a second-hand
book store, grading papers, *grading papers*, for days on end,
wearing—well, he doesn't seem to care what he wears. If he
feels like it, he just puts on the old striped tie with the plastic
neck band. You just snap the plastic band around your neck
and there the tie is, hanging down and ready to go, Pree-Tide.

—Tom Wolfe in the *New York Herald Tribune*,
November 1965

Score: 8—10—3

Comment: A good deal of the high jinks here is unmeasurable
by the machine, but it's pretty clear that Mr. Wolfe is working

over the reader strenuously. Astonishing number of noun adjuncts, some of them ironic. The structural details here that support a conversational tone are extreme, and entertaining: they include sheer breaks in the sentence like *wearing—well, he doesn't*. Point is that this is also the rhetoric of AROMA. The newspaper where this passage appeared and the newspaper represented by the previous sample (#9) have just announced that they are amalgamating. To the student of style this should come as no surprise.

Sample #11—Mostly Stuffy

In September 1959 there gathered at Woods Hole on Cape Cod some thirty-five scientists, scholars, and educators to discuss how education in science might be improved in our primary and secondary schools. The ten-day meeting had been called by the National Academy of Sciences, which through its Education Committee, had been examining for several years the long-range problem of improving the dissemination of scientific knowledge in America. The intention was not to institute a crash program, but rather to examine the fundamental processes involved in imparting to young students a sense of the substance and method of science.

—Jerome Bruner, *The Process of Education*
(1960), Preface

Score: 3—0—14

Comment: The machine is, I think, rather severe with this passage, which doesn't seem to my ear quite so Stuffy as all *that*. But the fact is that in category after category the prose here just manages to qualify: polysyllabic diction, neuter subjects, few verbs, noun adjuncts, plenty of subordination, and so on. Bruner's book has had an enormous influence on the educational establishment; perhaps, in its preface at any rate, it sounds a little too much like the establishment itself.

Sample #12—Mostly Stuffy

In agreement with the stipulation of the Terry Foundation that the lectures shall be concerned with "religion in the light of science and philosophy" I have chosen a concept in which theological, sociological, and philosophical problems converge, the concept of "courage." Few concepts are as useful for the analysis of the human situation. Courage is an ethical reality, but it is rooted in the whole breadth of human existence and ultimately in the structure of being itself. It must be considered ontologically in order to be understood ethically.

This becomes manifest in one of the earliest philosophical discussions of courage, in Plato's dialogue *Laches.*

—Paul Tillich, *The Courage To Be*
(1952), page 1

Score: 5—2—10

Comment: This theologian's effort to speak to an audience wider than his usual professional one is not altogether successful, or at any rate he has not avoided a high score in Stuffiness. Compare Samples 18 and 19, where similar efforts to reach popular audiences have been made, rather more Sweetly. The passage here is free from such Stuffy qualities as noun adjuncts and broken subject-verb patterns, but in other respects it makes the grade.

Sample #13—Mostly Stuffy

Warnings to many older persons not to over-exert themselves in activities such as snow-shoveling because of the heavy burden on the heart and blood circulation are frequently heard at this time of year. Often the stage for a heart attack has been set by years of little or no proper exercise. Doctors, therapists, and teachers dealing with health almost without exception recommend exercise to preserve health and youth as long as possible. The 1961 *Britannica Book of the Year* says, "The essence of living is action, and the normal state of body tissues is activity. It is evident that exercise is the master conditioner to keep the body healthy and one of the major therapeutic adjuncts to restoring health in the sick."

—from *Added Years: Newsletter of the New Jersey State Division on Aging* (January 1966)

Score: 6—3—11

Comment: We might expect such a simple message to be expressed in a folksy style, but evidently not so when a governmental hand starts fiddling with the rhetoric. The Stuffiness is fairly consistent throughout our categories, but is especially marked with respect to "self-embedding" structures —words intervening between subject and verb. In the first sentence above, there are 24 such words between *Warnings* and *are heard* (which by the way is passive). Such deliberation in coming to the point surely contributes to the remoteness of the voice in this passage. Can this be the appropriate style with which to persuade New Jersey's old folks to do their push-ups?

Sample #14—Mostly Stuffy

The idyllic harmony that suffuses Stifter's *Nachsommer* has been widely discussed and analyzed by scholars in the field, but less attention has been given to the undercurrent of sadness, which, in the words of Walter Rehm, is "hidden between the lines." A new dimension to our understanding of *Nach-sommer*—described by one writer as "inexhaustible in its mystery"—can indeed be added by further probing into the disturbances that lie beneath the smooth exterior of the novel.

The feeling of isolation experienced by the characters in *Nachsommer* presents an element of disquietude well worth exploring. As we trace this motif. . . .

—An article in PMLA (June 1965),
first paragraph

Score: 4—4—10

Comment: This scholarly opening of a scholarly article in a prestigious scholarly journal no doubt could be Stuffier, and the precise place where scholarship leaves off and pedantry begins is nothing I feel prepared to define. At any rate the most compelling figures for Stuffiness that the machine offers here are those for passive verbs and interrupted subject-verb combinations. Over half the verbs in this passage are in the passive voice, while almost every subject of a verb is immediately followed by modification and asides before the verb finally appears. These are the "self-embedding" structures discussed in Appendix A under Question 13, and on the whole they are not a kindness to the reader.

Sample #15—*Mostly Stuffy*

We feel the fundamental issue underlying the present discussion of social rules is the question of student maturity. Many of us feel that the administration's control of the judiciary system, curfew hours for women and permission for off-campus living discourage the exercise and development of social maturity which should be the right of every student.

It is our conviction that the student body is prepared to

exercise responsible self government and should be given the opportunity to play a decisive role in determining and enforcing rules pertaining to the general welfare of the student community. While these are certainly complex issues, this should not be used as an excuse for continued delay and inaction. All sides of the issue should be heard and every student be prepared to take a stand. Only when this is done will the administration be able to deal with student representatives and the true spokesmen for a mature student body.

—A Resolution by the Christian Association
of Swarthmore College, October 1965

Score: 5—1—12

Comment: A fine example of committee officialese composed by highly intelligent undergraduates at a first-rate liberal arts college. Most of the Stuffy weapons are here: heavy vocabulary, complex structures, endless subordinate clauses, noun adjuncts, passive verbs, and interrupted sentence patterns. The writers are aroused young people at war with their elders— and their prose style imitates their elders' least attractive face. If this is the wave of the future we are in trouble.

Sample #16—Mixed

In the recently published Life by Leslie Stephen of his brother, Fitz-James, there is an account of a school to which the latter went when he was a boy. The teacher, a certain Mr. Guest, used to converse with his pupils in this wise: "Gurney, what is the difference between justification and sanctification? —Stephen, prove the omnipotence of God!" etc. In the midst of our Harvard freethinking and indifference we are prone to imagine that here at your good old orthodox College conversation continues to be somewhat upon this order; and to show you that we at Harvard have not lost all interest in these vital subjects, I have brought with me tonight something like a sermon on justification *of* faith, a defence of our right to adopt a believing attitude in religious matters, in spite of the fact that our merely logical intellect may not have been coerced. "The Will to Believe," accordingly, is the title of my paper.

—William James, *The Will to Believe* (1896),
   opening lines

Score: 7—8—2

Comment: This beginning of a lecture on a pretty solemn subject (to a Philosophy Club at Yale) has been carefully phrased to keep an easy contact with the audience—that is, there are elements of Sweetness here. Even the punctuation is helpful in this respect: we have a question, an exclamation, a couple of dashes, an italicized *of*. The low score in Stuffiness is truly remarkable, considering the subject under discussion and the date of composition. I would like to see the modern theologian who could begin a lecture so gracefully and with so few Stuffy features of rhetoric.

Sample #17—Mixed

Strether's first question, when he reached the hotel, was about his friend; yet on his learning that Waymarsh was apparently not to arrive till evening he was not wholly disconcerted. A telegram from him bespeaking a room "only if not noisy," with the answer paid, was produced for the inquirer at the office, so that the understanding that they should meet at Chester rather than at Liverpool remained to that extent sound. The same secret principle, however, that had prompted Strether not absolutely to desire Waymarsh's presence at the dock, that had led him thus to postpone for a few hours his enjoyment of it, now operated to make him feel that he could wait without disappointment. They would dine together at the worst, and, with all respect to dear old Waymarsh—if not even, for that matter, to himself—there was little fear that in the sequel they should not see enough of each other.

> —Henry James, *The Ambassadors* (1903)

Score: 5—3—7

Comment: Nor is brother Henry to be classified as Stuffy, at least judging by this example of his late style. It is Stuffier than the opening of William's lecture (#16), and it depends for some of its heaviness on great generosity with subordinate clauses and James's characteristic willingness to introduce a subject, modify it and modify it again, then finally come through with a verb. (After *the same principle*, for instance, the reader must make his way through two fairly biggish clauses before finally reaching *operated*, the verb.) Nevertheless, the total effect here, at least as measured by the machine, is not excessively Stuffy, a fact which may reassure the reader who feels, beneath all the structural complexity, a warm and genial voice having fun with his narrative.

Sample #18—Mixed

Is love an art? Then it requires knowledge and effort. Or is love a pleasant sensation, which to experience is a matter of chance, something one "falls into" if one is lucky. This little book is based on the former premise, while undoubtedly the majority of people today believe in the latter.

Not that people think that love is not important. They are starved for it; they watch endless numbers of films about happy and unhappy love stories, they listen to hundreds of trashy songs about love—yet hardly anyone thinks that there is anything that needs to be learned about love.

—Erich Fromm, *The Art of Loving* (1956)

Score: 7—9—3

Comment: The effort to reach the reader directly is a little too energetic, and the result is a high score in Sweetness. A large number of finite verbs attest to the simplicity of the grammatical patterns. Modification is generous, and the punctuation is of the Sweet sort. By failing to address the reader as *you*, the style here falls just short of AROMA.

Sample #19—Mixed

This is a book of contrasts. I shall present a picture of two totally different kinds of neighborhoods and the public schools which serve them. I shall discuss city slums and wealthy suburbs. In the large metropolitan areas of New York, Philadelphia, Detroit, Chicago, and St. Louis, one has no difficulty in locating examples of both. In some cases twenty minutes' or half an hour's drive will enable a person to go from one to the other. A visit to the high school serving each community will open the eyes of a visitor to the complexities of American public education.

—J. B. Conant, *Slums and Suburbs* (1961)

Score: 7—8—4

Comment: This effort by a professional intellectual to reach a large audience is slightly less Sweet than Fromm's, and considerably less Stuffy than Tillich's (#12). Here there is a forthright *I* doing the talking, and his use of less than half the number of finite verbs we counted in #18 helps to reduce

the Sweetness by adding some complexity to sentence structure. The modification is Tough. The general difference may
be suggested by comparing *This is a book of contrasts* with the
slightly cute *this little book* of #18.

Sample #20—Mixed

Dear Investor:

When was the last time you received a thorough, impartial
analysis of your investment portfolio? Six months ago? A year
ago? Never?

At Merrill Lynch we believe that a periodic review of your
holdings is most important to the success of your investment
program. The securities you bought years ago or even months
ago may no longer be meeting your investment objective. The
outlook for the economy, the prospects for the stock market,
and the sundry factors affecting any particular security are
subject to change. Any of these changes can affect the stocks
you own.

> —Letter (unsolicited) received by the author,
> March 1966

Score: 5—8—3

Comment: This modified sales pitch is mixed indeed. In
vocabulary it is almost Stuffy, and the noun adjuncts are right
up to Stuffy standards. Yet the piece is more Sweet than anything else, of course, especially at the beginning. The stools
between which this style falls are that of the adman and that
of the academic economist. I venture to say that Merrill
Lynch's public ads would score slightly Sweeter than this
"letter," in which the individual recipient is being flattered
for his ability to take in elegant prose while at the same time

he is being loved up by direct address, sentence fragments, and the like. One difficulty with this document is that its reader, in the present case at any rate, is not now nor does he intend to be an Investor.

Sample #21—Mixed

The store in which the Justice of the Peace's court was sitting smelled of cheese. The boy, crouched on his nail keg at the back of the crowded room, knew he smelled cheese, and more: from where he sat he could see the ranked shelves close-packed with the solid, squat, dynamic shapes of tin cans whose labels his stomach read, not from the lettering which meant nothing to his mind but from the scarlet devils and the silver curve of fish—this, the cheese which he knew he smelled and the hermetic meat which his intestines believed he smelled coming in intermittent gusts momentary and brief between the other constant one, the smell and sense just a little of fear because mostly of despair and grief, the old fierce pull of blood.

—William Faulkner, "Barn Burning" (1939)

Score: 8—5—7

Comment: Very interesting mixture, with lush effects of Sweetness and Stuffiness to qualify the simplicity of the diction. (Four-fifths of these words are monosyllables!) Faulkner is generous with adjectives (Sweet) and with subordinate clauses (Stuffy); he is free with "self-embedding" structures (Stuffy); his repetitions of *the* are extraordinary (Tough). It is of course a very exciting style which fits no pat classification; the machine cannot touch whatever it is that holds this together.

Sample # 22—Mixed

I first met Dean not long after my wife and I split up. I had just gotten over a serious illness that I won't bother to talk about, except that it had something to do with the miserably weary split-up and my feeling that everything was dead. With the coming of Dean Moriarty began the part of my life you could call my life on the road. Before that I'd often dreamed of going West to see the country, always vaguely planning and never taking off. Dean is the perfect guy for the road because he actually was born on the road, when his parents were passing through Salt Lake City in 1926, in a jalopy, on their way to Los Angeles.

—Jack Kerouac, *On the Road* (1957)

Score: 8—6—5

Comment: This writing is exceedingly dreary; yet its score is actually not very far from that of Faulkner's intense language just preceding. It is another discouraging limitation of the style machine that it cannot distinguish between mixtures that are artful and mixtures that are just dull.

Sample #23—Mixed

In every day's newspaper there are stories about the two subjects that I have brought together in this book, the disgrace of the Organized System of semimonopolies, government, advertisers, etc., and the disaffection of the growing generation. Both are newsworthily scandalous, and for several years now both kinds of stories have come thicker and faster. It is strange that the obvious connections between them are not played up in the newspapers; nor, in the rush of books on the follies, venality, and stifling conformity of the Organization, has there been a book on Youth Problems in the organized System.

Those of the disaffected youth who are articulate, however —for instance, the Beat or Angry young men—are quite clear about the connection: their main topic is the "system" with which they refuse to co-operate.

—Paul Goodman, *Growing Up Absurd* (1960)

Score: 5—6—3

Comment: Mr. Goodman's Toughness is considerably weakened by heavy vocabulary, cumbersome sentence structure, and Sweet expressions like *newsworthily scandalous*. On the other hand, his reliance on forms of *to be* (7 out of 11 verbs) rivals Gertrude Stein's. The total effect seems to me Mixed in an unfavorable sense: the anger is muddled in journalism.

Sample #24—Mixed

When in the Course of human events it becomes necessary for one people to dissolve the political bands which have connected them with another, and to assume among the Powers of the earth, the separate and equal station to which the Laws of Nature and of Nature's God entitle them, a decent respect to the opinions of mankind requires that they should declare the causes which impel them to the separation.

We hold these truths to be self-evident, that all men are created equal, that they are endowed by their Creator with certain unalienable Rights, that among these are Life, Liberty and the pursuit of Happiness.

—The Declaration of Independence

Score: 5—3—8

Comment: Here is a piece of committee writing that fails to qualify as Stuffy. No noun adjuncts, not too many passives, a generous proportion of monosyllables, little interruption of subject and verb. It is true that the subordinate clause is used to the hilt: there's very little here that is *not* subordinated. Still, it is heartening to make the point that this admirable and admired piece of prose is indeed free of much of today's Stuffy qualities.

Sample #25—Mixed

Four score and seven years ago our fathers brought forth on this continent a new nation, conceived in Liberty, and dedicated to the proposition that all men are created equal.

Now we are engaged in a great civil war, testing whether that nation or any nation so conceived and so dedicated, can long endure. We are met on a great battle-field of that war. We have come to dedicate a portion of that field as a final resting place for those who here gave their lives that that nation might live. It is altogether fitting and proper that we should do this.

—The Gettysburg Address

Score: 7—8—4

Comment: Another exercise in patriotism. This is Sweeter than the Declaration, and less Stuffy, appropriately so for a speech addressed to a live audience. But its achievement, perhaps, is that it avoids all excesses, even Toughness.

These quick glances at eighteenth- and nineteenth-century style, written and spoken, suggest that the style machine might be useful in defining historical change. Though my essay has been primarily concerned with modern American prose, the opportunities for a chronological study are obvious.

NOTES

1. INTRODUCTIONS

1. I leave out of account, however, the situation, not after all unfamiliar, in which the two new acquaintances are of opposite sexes and promising ages—a situation that introduces its own patterns, of appalling complexity. How do I love thee? I may wish to count the ways, but even in the first five seconds of our acquaintance they are literally countless.

2. Visual ways of communicating (as opposed to verbal ways), known as *kinesics*, have received some attention from modern linguists, in spite of the obvious difficulties of description and classification. How many stages of the drooping eyelid can be identified? How many are meaningful, and to whom? For an introductory essay, see Ray L. Birdwhistell, "Kinesics and Communication," in Edmund Carpenter and Marshall McLuhan, eds., *Explorations in Communication* (Boston, 1960).

3. R. G. Collingwood made the point some years ago that vocal language is only one among many possible languages, any one of which might be developed by a particular civilization into a highly organized form of expression. "The cosmopolitan civilization of modern Europe and America . . . has limited our expressive activities almost entirely to the voice, and naturally tries to justify itself by asserting that the voice is the best medium for expression." (*The Principles of Art*, Oxford, 1938, pp. 244-45.)

4. Marshall McLuhan's well-known attack on the printed word (*Understanding Media*, New York, 1964) is even more sobering. In an electronic age, says McLuhan, where "the me-

dium is the message," the time-sequence basic to printing becomes increasingly irrelevant.

5. See Wayne Booth, *The Rhetoric of Fiction* (Chicago, 1961), pp. 70-73 and passim. This influential work on the narrator in fiction is referred to again, more adequately, in Chapter 5. Also see Kathleen Tillotson, *The Tale and the Teller* (London, 1959).

6. An earlier statement of this argument, with various examples, appears in my "Authors, Speakers, Readers, and Mock Readers," *College English*, XI (February, 1950), 265-69. The term "mock reader" for the reader's second self now seems to me misleading. Would ideal reader be better? Expected reader? Assumed reader? The assumed reader of this essay, that sympathetic fellow, has grasped the general idea with his usual acumen. Yes, he says, yes yes, go on.

2. HEARING VOICES

1. *Saturday Review*, XLIV (January 7, 1961). The author is Mr. Harold Taylor.

2. This has of course absolutely nothing to do—or almost nothing to do—with the writer as an actual person. See Chapter 1 and the distinction between real-life author and assumed author.

3. *Saturday Review*, XXXIII (November 4, 1950). By Irwin Edman.

4. David H. Stevens, *The Changing Humanities* (New York, 1953), p. 173. Title added.

5. *The Critic*, XVIII (1960). By T. S. Eliot.

3. TOUGH TALK

1. Ernest Hemingway, *A Farewell to Arms* (New York, 1929). Used by permission of the publishers, Charles Scribner's Sons.

2. It would have been possible for Hemingway to insist on even more mock-knowledge of what-was-said-before-the-story-started. He could have written, "We lived in the house in the village that looked across the river. . . ." In that case the assumed

reader would have to further assume that he knew which house it was—that particular one (of course!) that looked across the river.

3. *A Farewell to Arms,* page 191. Used by permission of the publishers, Charles Scribner's Sons.

4. DULLNESS AND DISHONESTY

1. *New York Review of Books,* VI 1 (February 3, 1966). The same issue contains an attack by Dwight Macdonald on "parajournalism" as exemplified by the prose of Tom Wolfe in the *Herald Tribune.* "Parajournalism" is also essentially a mixture of genres, where presumably factual information is uttered by the all-knowing voice of the novel. Under such circumstances, as Mr. Macdonald shows, you don't have to worry much about evidence.

2. In newswriting, the substitution for a conventional newspaper headline of a *title,* à la fiction or an expository article of comment, is a step toward the pose of omniscience. The *Times'* article was headlined "Rioting Negroes Routed by Police at Birmingham"; the *Tribune*'s was *called* "Birmingham's Trigger Tension." An event becomes a topic, a subject, a *thing.* The use of alliteration in titles may be further cause for suspicion on the part of a wary reader. See also Chapter 6, where a relation between naming and omniscience is observed in the style of advertising.

5. FREE STYLE

1. Saul Bellow, *The Adventures of Augie March* (New York, 1953). Published by Viking Press.

2. These remarks help to explain why Bellow's later *Herzog* (1964) is a more successful book, indeed a brilliant and altogether satisfying one. In *Herzog* the narrator slides easily in and out of the hero's own language, and we know pretty well which is which. Herzog himself is wonderfully self-aware and articulate: "that suffering joker," he calls himself, and at that we laugh at him and laugh with him and suffer too with him in a combination that seems to be truly controlled.

3. Robert Penn Warren, *All the King's Men* (New York, 1946). Published by Harcourt, Brace, and World.

4. Is it reassuring or is it irritating to discover that someone else has already expressed one's ingenious discovery? In this case, at any rate, someone has. Roger Sale, in an article on Warren in the *Hudson Review* (XIV 1, Spring 1961), contrasts Jack Burden with Marlowe, the thoroughgoing, unambiguous tough guy of Raymond Chandler's mysteries. Marlowe, Sale says, "does not try to protect himself by anticipating the reader's irony. Jack constantly hedges his bet, talks down but then dissociates himself from the consequences." The result is an "embarrassing collocation of the tough guy with the lover of truth and mountain brooks." I hasten to say, with the anxiety customary in such cases, that I was led to this fine article after I had composed my interpretation of Jack Burden.

5. Wright Morris, *Love among the Cannibals* (New York, 1957). Published by Harcourt Brace and Company.

6. J. D. Salinger, *Franny and Zooey* (Boston, 1961). Published by Little Brown and Company.

7. Anxiety about language is one thing; downright hostility is something else. An author who really believes that silence is more golden than words is not likely to inspire confidence in the fruits of his authorship. And he has a built-in excuse for his own shortcomings. As Benjamin DeMott has recently put it, "the writer who takes up the theme of silence as glory (or speechmaking as sin) enjoys cosy immunity from the start. Words are the one means of justifying the contention that language is the foe of honesty and reality: how then can you expect a word-hater to explain his hatred?" *You Don't Say* (New York, 1966), pp. 56-57.

8. Hayden Carruth, *Appendix A* (New York, 1963). This passage and that in the Style Sampler (Sample #6) used by permission of the publisher, The Macmillan Company.

6. SWEET TALK

1. Marshall McLuhan believes that these nonverbal resources are more important to an ad's effect than anything words can say.

"Since the advent of pictures, the job of the ad copy is as inci-
dental and latent, as the 'meaning' of a poem is to a poem, or
the words of a song are to a song. Highly literate people cannot
cope with the nonverbal art of the pictorial, so they dance impa-
tiently up and down to express a pointless disapproval that
renders them futile and gives new power and authority to the
ads. The unconscious depth-messages of ads are never attacked
by the literate, because of their incapacity to notice or discuss
nonverbal forms of arrangement and meaning. They have not
the art to argue with pictures." *Understanding Media* (New
York, 1964), p. 231.

2. The development I have described here is accelerating.
According to *The New York Times* (January 17, 1966), the
year 1965 saw increased sophistication in advertising, largely
because the industry "even poked a little fun at itself." "Humor
played an important role in the evolution of advertising last
year, with much of it fresh and original." A good deal of the
credit is generally granted to the firm of Doyle Dane Bernbach,
Inc., authors of the admirable Volkswagen and Avis ads, both of
which sell their products by pretending to knock them.

Recent adwriting may also be related to a distinction Susan
Sontag has enunciated, between style and stylization. " 'Stylization' in a work of art," she writes, "as distinct from style, reflects
an ambivalence (affection contradicted by contempt, obsession
contradicted by irony) toward the subject-matter. This ambivalence is handled by maintaining, through the rhetorical overlay
that is stylization, a special distance from the subject. But the
common result is that either the work of art is excessively narrow
and repetitive, or else the different parts seem unhinged, disso-
ciated . . . . it is evident that stylized art, palpably an art of
excess, lacking harmoniousness, can never be of the very greatest
kind." Susan Sontag, *Against Interpretation* (New York, 1966),
p. 20.

7. STUFFY TALK

1. Actually, in various works on the subject, there has been
precious little sympathy for the writers of officialese, who are an

easy mark for critical abuse. Among numerous discussions of official style, all fairly bloodthirsty, I recommend: George Orwell's famous essay, "Politics and the English Language," in *Shooting an Elephant and Other Essays* (1950), Robert Graves and Alan Hodge, *The Reader over your Shoulder* (1946), and Robert Waddell, *Grammar and Style* (1951), which contains an entertaining "grammar of Basic Jargon." See also, for an earlier attack, Sir Arthur Quiller-Couch, *On the Art of Writing* (1916).

2. In the version published in book form, the following prefatory remark describes the intention in this section of the report: "Realizing that for the convenience of all types of serious readers it would be desirable to simplify language, condense chapters, and bring opinions to the forefront, the Committee offers Part I as such a presentation." *Smoking and Health*, Public Health Service Publication No. 1103, U. S. Government Printing Office, p. 5.

3. The pussyfooting language seems at odds with the conviction about *cause* that the Committee evidently did feel. The book version of the report contains a statement about this conviction, after some cautious warning about the Committee's use of the word "cause." "No member was so naive as to insist upon mono-etiology in pathological processes or in vital phenomena." Nevertheless, "granted these complexities were recognized, it is to be noted clearly that the Committee's considered decision to use the words 'a cause,' or 'a major cause,' or 'a significant cause,' or 'a causal association' in certain conclusions about smoking and health affirms their conviction." (*Smoking and Health*, p. 21.) What interests me here is that this conviction is affirmed in language that almost removes the affirmers from the scene.

4. Extraordinary efforts, over the past quarter century and more, have been devoted by psychologists and others to devising formulas for measuring "readability." The best-known of these formulas are those constructed by Rudolph Flesch (*The Art of Plain Talk*, etc.). Readability, or Reading Ease (Flesch's term), refers entirely to the comfort and efficiency of the reader in "understanding" the words in front of him. Most of the formulas proposed to measure this quality depend heavily on simple

computations of sentence length and word length. These formulas, as their inventors usually concede, are not concerned with *style* in my sense, as the expression of a personality on paper. No doubt such formulas may be helpful to some writers in improving style—especially the style of Stuffy Talk—but the experts in readability are not worried about what happens to the voice when their formulas are applied. See George R. Klare, *The Measurement of Readability* (Ames, Iowa, 1963).

5. But see Sample #24 in the Style Sampler, Appendix B.

8. BEING SERIOUS WITHOUT BEING STUFFY

1. The three passages in this chapter were taken from prefaces of the following anthologies: Leonard F. Dean and Kenneth G. Wilson, *Essays on Language and Usage* (New York, 1959); John A. Rycenga and Joseph Schwartz, *Perspectives on Language* (New York, 1963); Donald W. Lee, *English Language Reader* (New York, 1963). These passages have been scored for Toughness-Sweetness-Stuffiness in accordance with the style machine described in my appendix. The first passage checks in at 9 points for Toughness, 5 for Sweetness, and 5 for Stuffiness. The second scores 3 - 1 - 10 respectively, and the third 3 - 3 - 10. I think those figures may fairly well suggest the distinction in tone experienced by the reader of the three passages.

APPENDIX A

1. In *Enemies of Promise* (1938), Cyril Connolly speaks of "the new relationship with the reader which is to sweep over the twentieth century and dominate journalism and advertising. It may be described as *you*-writing from the fact that there is a constant tendency to harangue the reader in the second person. It is a buttonholing approach." Connolly calls this style "the New Vernacular," and he distinguishes it from the ornate, traditional "Mandarin" style, "characterised by long sentences with many dependent clauses, by the use of the subjunctive and conditional, by exclamations and interjections, quotations, allu-

sions, metaphors, long images, Latin terminology, subtlety, and conceits." I suppose that in this study I have discriminated between two kinds of Vernacular (Tough and Sweet), while my Stuffy Talk is a dreadful parody of the Mandarin grand manner. Meanwhile, the flexible style Connolly appeals for, a combination of Mandarin and Vernacular, may possibly be visible in some of the Mixed items in my Style Sampler of Appendix B.

For another, and more recent, attempt to classify styles, see Martin Joos, *The Five Clocks* (Bloomington, 1963). Considering oral speech as well as written language, Joos distinguishes five styles. His labels for them are: frozen, formal, consultative, casual, and intimate.

2. I have made some effort in this study to use the pattern approach to sentence structure to which the structural linguists have been introducing us for some years. However, except for the clear difference in the use of the passive voice of the verb (what is often called Sentence Pattern 5 and 6), I found not enough difference in sentence pattern among my styles to warrant including the figures. It is evidently possible to sound Tough or Sweet or Stuffy in any sentence pattern, as "pattern" is defined by the new grammarian. (The transformational approach, on the other hand, seems likely to offer some genuine opportunities for further classification.) As for the passive voice, I consider that important difference in my next question, where I use the traditional vocabulary.

3. C. C. Fries, *American English Grammar* (New York, 1940), p. 98.

4. Educationese seems to be particularly afflicted. The notorious conflict between colleges of liberal arts and colleges of education, like many conflicts, is fought by means of crucial differences in prose style, and the educationist is characteristically more generous with his noun adjuncts. Battle lines are clearly drawn in a recent article by Reuben A. Brower, who is firmly in the camp of the liberal arts. Professor Brower does not use the term "noun adjunct," but the distinction appears in his very title, "Book Reading and the Reading of Books," where *book reading* is condemned and *the reading of books* is defended. Of the prose style of the educationist, Brower says: "We may for-

give the flatness in the interest of objectivity, but not the Germanic compounds of which 'book reading' is a mild example. We hear too often: 'language skills,' 'reading skills,' 'recognition skills,' 'content fields,' and 'content analysis'; and too many plurals such as 'language immaturities,' 'these learnings,' and 'these recognitions.' A climactic sentence in one report ends with: 'the desired pupil learning outcomes.' " Roger H. Smith, ed., *The American Reading Public* (New York, 1963), pp. 23-24.

5. Fries, *American English Grammar*, p. 274.

6. Otto Jespersen, *Modern English Grammar*, Vol. III (Heidelberg, 1927), pp. 132-153.

7. Richard Ohmann has summarized the distinction clearly in an article in *Word* (December, 1964): "It has often been pointed out that constructions may be left-branching ('Once George had left, the host and hostess gossiped briskly'), right-branching ('The host and hostess gossiped briskly, once George had left'), or self-embedding ('The host and hostess, once George had left, gossiped briskly'). Neither left- nor right-branching constructions tax the hearer's understanding, even when compounded at some length ('a very few not at all well liked union officials'; 'the dog that worried the cat that chased the rat that ate the cheese that lay in the house that Jack built'). But layers of self-embedding quickly put too great a strain on the unaided memory ('the house in which the cheese that the rat that the cat that the dog worried chased ate lay was built by Jack'). Even a relatively small amount of self-embedding in a written passage can slow a reader down considerably."

8. See note 1, Chapter 6.

INDEX